The

Reminiscences

of

Vice Admiral Olaf M. Hustvedt

U. S. Navy (Retired)

U. S. Naval Institute
Annapolis, Maryland

1975

PREFACE

This volume contains the transcript of ten taped interviews with Vice Admiral Olaf M. Hustvedt, U. S. Navy (Ret.). The interviews were conducted by John T. Mason, Jr. for the Oral History Office of the U. S. Naval Institute and were held in the home of Admiral Hustvedt on Ordway Street in Washington, D. C. They cover a period ranging from November 29, 1973 to June 11, 1974.

Admiral Hustvedt has made minor corrections in the transcript and it has been re-typed, but essentially it remains as spoken by him on tape.

A subject index has been added for convenience. A copy of an earlier interview given by the Admiral to several representatives of the National Air and Space Museum of the Smithsonian Institution has been included in the appendix.

Admiral Hustvedt's career was concerned with Naval Ordnance over a long span with several tours of duty as head of the Experimental Section in the Bureau of Ordnance (dating back as far as 1919) and with another as Production Chief of the Naval Gun Factory (1930). In addition, the Admiral had considerable experience in Battleships dating from World War I. His final tour of duty was in Command of Battleship Division 7 with the Fast Carrier Task Force in the Pacific (World War II).

John T. Mason, Jr.
Director of Oral History
U. S. Naval Institute

May, 1975

VICE ADMIRAL OLAF M. HUSTVEDT, U. S. NAVY, RETIRED

Olaf Mandt Hustvedt was born in Chicago, Illinois, on June 23, 1886. He attended public schools and Luther College at Decorah, Iowa, before his appointment to the U. S. Naval Academy, Annapolis, Maryland, from the Fourth District of Iowa in 1905. While a Midshipman he played football, commanded the Company which won the Brigade Colors, and was on the "Lucky Bag" Committee. Graduated with distinction, eighth in his class, in June 1909, he served the two years at sea, then required by law, and was commissioned Ensign, USN, on June 5, 1911. He was promoted to Lieutenant (jg) on June 5, 1914, and to Lieutenant and Lieutenant Commander during World War I, and subsequently attained the rank of Rear Admiral, to date from November 20, 1941 (temporary) and from June 30, 1942 (permanent). He was advanced to the rank of Vice Admiral upon his retirement on March 1, 1945, on the basis of combat citation during World War II.

After graduation from the Naval Academy in June 1909, he served in the USS WEST VIRGINIA and USS RALEIGH until September 1912, then had instruction in the Bureau of Ordnance, Navy Department, Washington, D. C., and at George Washington University in that city, receiving the degree of Master of Science in 1914. In September of that year he joined the USS UTAH, and in June 1916 was transferred to duty as Aide on the Staff of Commander Battleship Division 6, Atlantic Fleet. That Division operated with the British Grand Fleet during the first World War, and for his services, he was awarded a Special Letter of Commendation from the Navy Department, stating: "He performed meritorious service as Flag Secretary on the Staff of Battleship Division SIX, U. S. Atlantic Fleet."

In November 1918 he joined the USS OKLAHOMA, in which he served as Gunnery Officer until January 1919, when he was ordered to the Bureau of Ordnance, Navy Department. There he served until May 1922 as Chief of the Experimental Section. When detached he was ordered to Mine Squadron TWO, Pacific Fleet, based at Pearl Harbor, T. H., and had command of the USS BURNS from July of that year until December 1924. Upon his return to the United States, he again served as Chief of the Experimental Section, Bureau of Ordnance, after which, in May 1927, he became Gunnery Officer of the USS COLORADO.

A year later he reported as Aide and Divisions Gunnery Officer on the Staff of Vice Admiral Louis M. Nulton, USN, then Commander Battleship Divisions, Battle Fleet, the USS WEST VIRGINIA, flagship. From May 1929 to June 1930 he served as Fleet Gunnery Officer on the Staff, when Admiral Nulton was Commander in Chief, Battle Fleet, his flag in the USS CALIFORNIA. He returned to shore duty in August 1930, serving until May 1933 at the Naval Gun Factory, U. S. Navy Yard, Washington, D. C. He next served as Executive Officer of the USS LOUISVILLE, and when detached in June 1935, began a three year tour of duty in the Office of the Chief of Naval Operations, Navy Department, with duty part of that time as Director of the Central Division.

From July 1938 until April 1939 he commanded the USS DETROIT, and for ten months thereafter served as Operations Officer on the Staff of the Commander in Chief, U. S. Fleet, in the USS PENNSYLVANIA, flagship. In January 1940 he again reported to the Office of the Chief of Naval Operations, serving briefly before reporting to the Naval War College, Newport, Rhode Island, where he was a student until June 1940. He next had duty fitting out the USS NORTH CAROLINA, building at the New York Navy Yard, and assumed command of that battleship on her commissioning, April 9, 1941.

V. Adm. Olaf M. Hustvedt, USN, Ret.

On October 23, 1941, he was transferred to duty as Chief of Staff and Aide to the Commander in Chief, U. S. Atlantic Fleet. For his service during the early period of World War II, he was awarded the Legion of Merit, with citation to follow:

"For exceptionally meritorious conduct in the performance of outstanding services to the Government of the United States as Chief of Staff to the Commander in Chief, U. S. Atlantic Fleet, during the period October 25, 1941 to May 4, 1943. Intimately concerned with all activities of the Atlantic Fleet, Rear Admiral Hustvedt rendered invaluable assistance in the exacting task of organizing the Fleet and its bases and in establishing sound command relationship in the early months of the war. His judicious counsel and clear perception in escort of convoy and anti-submarine operational problems contributed vitally to the success conduct of Fleet operations in the Western Atlantic Area."

In May 1943 he became Commander Battleships, Atlantic Fleet, with additional duty in command of Battleship Division 5, later Battleship Division 7. While in that command, he had additional duty in command of two separate United States Task Groups which operated with the British Home Fleet in European waters from May to August 1943 and from September to September to November 1943, respectively. In December 1943 his Division of Battleships was deployed to the Pacific Combat Area, and he remained in command until October 1944. For "exceptionally meritorious conduct...as Commander of a Battleship Division in action against enemy Japanese forces in the Truk Island Area on February 16-17, and in the vicinity of Saipan, Tinian and Guam Islands, February 21-22, 1944..." he was awarded a Gold Star in lieu of the Second Legion of Merit, with Combat "V." The citation further states:

"A forceful and inspiring leader, Rear Admiral Hustvedt consistently directed the operations of his division skillfully and with aggressive determination during vital carrier raids against the enemy in these highly strategic areas. When his task force was subjected to a series of fierce Japanese aerial torpedo and bombing strikes, lasting throughout the night of February 21 and into the following morning, the ships under his command fought valiantly and contributed to the destruction of two hostile planes, thereby assisting the task group in reaching the initial launching point and delivering a devastating air attack on Japanese aircraft, shipping and shore installations which resulted in heavy enemy losses. By his expert tactical control and steadfast devotion to duty under extremely difficult conditions, Rear Admiral Hustvedt brought his division through these engagements without damage and materially aided our forces in the successful completion of their missions."

Returning to the United States, he reported on December 4, 1944, as a Member of the General Board, Navy Department, Washington, D. C. He served there, after his transfer to the Retired List on March 1, 1945, throughout the remaining period of the war and until April 1946, when he was relieved of all active duty.

In addition to the Legion of Merit and Gold Star in lieu of the Second Legion of Merit, with Combat "V," Vice Admiral Hustvedt has the Victory Medal, Grand Fleet Clasp; the American Defense Service Medal, Fleet Clasp; American Campaign Medal; European-African-Middle Eastern Campaign Medal; Asiatic-Pacific Campaign Medal; and the World War II Victory Medal.

V. Adm. Olaf M. Hustvedt, USN, Ret. Page 3

He also has been awarded the decoration, Commander of the Military Division, Most Excellent Order of the British Empire, by the Government of Great Britain.

Admiral Hustvedt, with his wife, the former Irene Sherwood Cooper of Honolulu, Hawaii, reside at 3525 Ordway Street, Northwest, Washington, D. C. They have three children: Their daughter, Virginia, is the wife of Captain Philip F. Hauck, USN. One son, Erling Halvor Hustvedt, was an officer in the U. S. Naval Reserve during World War II, and the other son, Stephen Roald Hustvedt served as an officer in the Army of the United States, with Army Occupation Forces in the European Theater after the war.

Navy Office of Information
Biographies Branch
29 March 1962

DECLARATION OF TRUST

The undersigned does hereby appoint and designate as his (her) Trustee herein, the Secretary-Treasurer and Publisher of the United States Naval Institute to perform and discharge the following duties, powers, and privileges in connection with the possession and use of a certain taped interview between the undersigned and the Oral History Department of the United States Naval Institute.

1. Classification of Transcript.

   (✓)a. If classified <u>OPEN</u>, the transcript(s) may be read or the recording(s) audited by the qualified personnel upon presentation of proper credentials, as determined by the Secretary-Treasurer of the U. S. Naval Institute.

   ( )b. If classified <u>PERMISSION REQUIRED TO CITE OR QUOTE</u>, the user will be required to obtain permission in writing from the interviewee prior to quoting or citing from either the transcript(s) or the recording(s).

   ( )c. If classified <u>PERMISSION REQUIRED</u>, permission must be obtained in writing from the interviewee before the transcribed interview(s) can be examined or the tape recording(s) audited.

   ( )d. If classified <u>CLOSED</u>, the transcribed interview(s) and the tape recording(s) will be sealed until a time specified by the interviewee. This may be until the death of the interviewee or for any specified number of years.

   It is expressly understood that in giving this authorization, I am in no way precluded from placing such restrictions as I may desire upon use of the interview at any time during my lifetime, nor does this authorization in any way affect my rights to the copyright of my literary expressions that may be contained in the interview.

Witness my hand and seal this 2nd day of April 1975.

_____

I hereby accept and consent to the foregoing Declaration of Trust and the powers therein conferred upon me as Trustee:

_____

Interview No. 1 with Vice Admiral Olaf M. Hustvedt, U.S. Navy
(Retired)

Place: His residence in Washington, D.C.

Date: Thursday morning, 29 November 1973

Subject: Biography

By: John T. Mason, Jr.

Q: Admiral, I've heard so very much about you from various people. You're almost a legendary figure, you know. I'm delighted, therefore, that you will give us a series of interviews covering your very significant naval career.

Inasmuch as this is a biography, a talking biography if you will, I wonder if you'd begin in the traditional way by telling me where you were born, when you were born, and something about your background?

Adm. H.: I'd be glad to. I was born in Chicago, Illinois, in June of 1886. So far as personal background is concerned, my forebears were all Norwegians. They were pioneers in the Middle West. My paternal grandparents came to this country as very young people. My grandmother, I think, at the age of six or seven, and my grandfather at the age of nineteen, both in the early 1840s. They were in Wisconsin — I'm not sure whether Wisconsin was a state or territory at that time. They were in Wisconsin in the early 1840s. I think Wisconsin was just about becoming a state at that time. Gold had not yet been discovered in California.

Q: So they stopped there?

Adm. H.: Well, they were too young to be thinking of gold, I think. At any rate, they two, my father's parents, were both born in Telemark in Norway. Incidentally, Telemark is known for being the birthplace of skiing, perhaps, and it may be of interest to remark that a first cousin of my father who was born in Telemark became a ski-jump champion in Norway, and his life and career more or less connected with skiing from then on. He was a member of Amundsen's South Pole expedition. He was the ski expert, and Amundsen in his book on the South Pole discovery recounts that on the last day's trek, when he knew that the immediate vicinity of the pole would be reached that day, put Olaf Bjaaland, his skier, into the lead, so that putatively you might say that Olaf Bjaaland, my father's first cousin, was the first man at the South Pole.

Well, that goes back into connections rather far.

Q: What did the family do in Wisconsin? Was it dairying and that sort of thing?

Adm. H.: No. In those days, in Wisconsin, of course, they

were immigrants who came to the United States to acquire land, and that's what they did. They acquired land.

My mother's parents came from Norway a little later than that and also acquired land in that same part of Wisconsin. By a curious coincidence, you might say, although my mother and father were born on farms about four miles apart in Wisconsin they never met until my father was in college in Iowa. My mother's brother was a teacher at the college. I think that's a curious set of circumstances.

Q: They weren't quite as mobile as we are!

Adm. H.: No, I should say not. And, incidentally, referring to the mobility of those early days, when my father went from southern Wisconsin to northeastern Iowa to go to college, he went by rail as far as Prairie du Chin, Wisconsin, where there was as yet no bridge. So he went with a small group of lads from his own neighborhood and, after being ferried across the Mississippi at Prairie du Chien, they were able to hire a farmer with a wagon on the other side who hauled their baggage the rest of the way, which was forty-odd miles to Decorah, Iowa, where the college was located.

Q: What college is that?

Adm. H.: Luther College. And the prospective students trudged alongside the wagon forty miles from Prairie du Chien to Decorah, while their baggage rode.

Q: I think they were a little more rugged than we are!

Adm. H.: Yes, well, those were pioneer days, of course.

Q: I think the remarkable thing is, Admiral, that they sought a college education. Was this a tradition in the family?

Adm. H.: I have no doubt that it was a tradition to seek a good education, but as far as I know, there were no university graduates on either side.

I have mentioned my father's first cousin Bjaaland, who was the ski expert and afterwards became a manufacturer of skis in Oslo, but there was a tradition of education behind those people. In Norwegian literature there is a big name that is probably very little known in this country. This country knows a great deal about Ibsen and Bjornson and various others, but the name of Vinje not very well known in the United States. But Vinje was a big literary figure in the Norway of his time, and his family were neighbors in Telemark of my grandfather's family. I'm not sure whether there was a family connection or not, but they came from the same immediate neighborhood. So people there were very literate, although they didn't perhaps get to a university, very many of them. Back in the early days of the nineteenth century I don't suppose there were many from that area who actually went to colleges. But in this country they were quick to establish their institutions, including a college. This institution that I'm speaking of in Decorah, Iowa, was a college established in

1861, although those were troubled times. They established a college there which flourishes to this day, and it has a very high reputation, incidentally.

Q: Yes. So your father went there to college and prepared himself for what kind of a career?

Adm. H.: For the ministry, actually. That was the principal purpose of that college. Not to serve as a theological seminary but to serve as an institution for the education of young men in the classics. The course that was established there - and it was a one-course institution for a great many years - was highly classical. I can remember, for instance, that when I went from Luther College to the Naval Academy we were engaged in reading the Medea of Euripides, when I left school, and we were engaged in studying the French Revolution. We had finished our mathematics and our physics and, at the time I went to the Naval Academy, I had studied in three modern languages and two dead languages. English, of course, was my mother tongue, Norwegian by inheritance. I didn't regard myself as particularly expert in Norwegian, but I had had all of my religious instruction in Norwegian. We had courses at the college in Norwegian literature. At the college I studied German for four years, including my preparatory department years. I studied Latin for four years, Greek for three years.

Q: So you were reading Medea in Greek?

Hustvedt # 1 - 6

Adm. H.: Oh, yes. Yes, indeed. That's the last Greek that I remember from that Course. Of course, we had begun more or less with Xenophon, then the Odyssey and the Iliad. I think every second year student of Greek probably deals with Homer, after he's learned to read it a bit. But the Medea was the last thing that I can remember in Greek. Latin, I think we were in Virgil. But you don't want all of this!

Q: It's very interesting as a background. I should imagine there were very few young men going to the Naval Academy with this kind of a background?

Adm. H.: Oh, I daresay that there were very, very few.

Q: Did your father then become an active clergyman?

Adm. H.: Yes. He was a pioneer clergyman in South Dakota, in the neighborhood of Yankton, and later on in Iowa, at Northwood. He was forced to leave active ministry shortly before I was born on account of a throat affliction that made it very hard for him to preach. But during the rest of his life he was still connected with the church organization as their national treasurer, as head of a church normal school, and as editor of church publications. He was in that sort of church activity all of his active life.

Q: This was the Norwegian Lutheran Church?

Adm. H.: This was what is now known as the American Lutheran

Church. It was then known as the Norwegian Evangelical Lutheran Church because they, I suppose naturally, clung to their Norwegian connection for quite a long time, but the Norwegian tag no longer is used. It's now the American Lutheran Church.

Q: I suppose the facility with the Norwegian language has been lost, too, in many of the families?

Adm. H.: Oh, yes. The Norwegian language was used in the church services for years. At the time I was a youngster living at home, English had been introduced in the church, but the principal service - the Sunday forenoon service - was still conducted in Norwegian. Other services were conducted in English and, of course, now the Norwegian has disappeared. I can't put a time tag on that, but it disappeared during my lifetime.

Q: So you grew up in this atmosphere, a very scholarly background, and a religious one?

Adm. H.: I think it's fair to say that, yes.

Q: What were your intentions in going to Luther College? Did you plan to go into the ministry, too?

Adm. H.: No. I rather definitely planned not to, but I had not fixed my intentions on anything definite. I was still pretty young, of course. I was between eighteen and nineteen when I went to the Academy, but I was fairly well settled that

I was not going into the ministry.

Q: Was your father unhappy at this prospect?

Adm. H.: At my not going into the ministry? No. No, I think he realized that his calling was not necessarily the calling of his sons - he had four sons, and the eldest did go into the ministry, incidentally. But the eldest left the ministry and went into teaching. He became a teacher of English, as I remember, at the University of Illinois, then the University of Minnesota, and finally the University of California at Los Angeles. He was a part of the original faculty at UCLA and was a full professor at UCLA at the time of his retirement. Incidentally, he became a very highly respected authority on ballad literature because he was able to read Norwegian, he was able to read Danish, if you will, Swedish, Finnish, any of the Scandinavian languages, to say nothing of German. He wrote a couple of books on the topic of ballad literature in all of those northern languages.

Q: Fascinating!

Adm. H.: He became, I think, of his time possibly the foremost authority in this country on ballad literature in the Germanic languages. Professor Child of Harvard, I think, was preeminent in that field during his time and my brother studied with him, incidentally.

That was digression, wasn't it?

Hustvedt #1 - 9

Q: Yes, but I wanted to ask how you arrived at the idea that you wanted to go to the Naval Academy?

Adm. H.: That was accidental. An uncle of mine was a member of the faculty at Luther College during most of his adult life, and he had been nominated as the Democratic candidate for Congress from our home district in the campaign of 1892.

Q: This was Wisconsin?

Adm. H.: No, Decorah, Iowa, Luther College. That's where I grew up. I didn't grow up in Wisconsin, I grew up in Decorah, Iowa, where my father had been sent to college.

Q: And where your uncle was on the staff.

Adm. H.: And my uncle was a member of the faculty for a great many years. While he was a member of the faculty he was nominated by the Democrats for Congress in the campaign of 1892. Well, the campaign of 1892 was one in which the Democrats won, but in the Fourth District of Iowa my uncle lost.

Q: That was the Cleveland campaign?

Adm. H.: That was Cleveland, and presumably as a reward for having put up a good fight he was appointed consul general to Rotterdam by President Cleveland. He served as such in

Rotterdam during the Cleveland administration, but when McKinley came in in 1896 there was a change in the office of consul general at Rotterdam and my uncle came back to Luther College. That uncle was my mother's brother. His name was Reque.

Well, Professor Reque was in town one day in spring when he ran across the local congressman, whose name was Haugen, and that name has gone down in history, more or less.

Q: Gilbert Haugen?

Adm. H.: Gilbert N. Haugen.

Q: Yes, I knew him.

Adm. H.: Did you? From Northwood, Iowa. Where did you know him, here in Washington? Yes, Haugen appointed me to the Academy.

Q: Oh, he did, really?

Adm. H.: Yes, it came about in this way. My uncle, L. S. Reque, was in town one day and ran across Congressman Haugen on the street in Decorah, Iowa, where I grew up and went to college and all that. They knew each other and they stopped and talked and, as they parted, Mr. Haugen said, "Incidentally, Reque, I'm looking for candidates for the Naval Academy. You have a son that's about the right age, haven't you?" Well, as they discussed it, they found that my cousin was not of the right age because he was just about to turn twenty, but my uncle said, "I have a nephew here who might be right for you." So that's the way I was appointed to the Naval Academy!

Q: How did your parents react to this?

Adm. H.: They liked it.

Q: Of course, Norwegians are seafaring people.

Adm. H.: The idea was new to my parents and new to me, but it was perfectly agreeable all around.

Q: So you took the examination and came?

Adm. H.: I took the examination as an alternate and didn't make the grade, but Mr. Haugen gave me a similar appointment as an alternate in the spring of 1905, and I passed. The principal appointee did not pass, so I wound up at the Naval Academy. Sort of a long shot!

Q: How interesting. Tell me about your impressions of the Academy and the life there.

Adm. H.: Well, I was somewhat prepared for it because, although I had not given it any thought as being something in my life, at the time this alternate appointment came out of the blue, I had developed a very strong interest in the Navy, as most of my contemporaries did on account of the campaigns of 1898. In those days, boys, at least in my area, in my town, there were boys who collected pictures of warships the way people collect stamps. I had a warship collection when I was twelve years old, during the Spanish War, and I wasn't the only one in my neighborhood or in my school. It was a fad..

So going to the Naval Academy appealed to me when it was put up.

Q: Did you find the intellectual life at the Academy somewhat different from Luther College?

Adm. H.: The courses of study, of course, were far different. I had rather an inadequate background in math, because, in shifting from a public high school to the Luther College prep department, I missed a certain amount of algebra, because the college boys went a little faster in algebra in the prep department than we did in the high school. So when I became a prep at Luther I was ready for the final year of the prep department but there was a gap in my math in the algebra section.

Well, that plagued me a little, but I got over it. Of course, at the Naval Academy our algebra consisted of about an initial month of polishing in plebe class and we went on to other things.

Q: But other than that, in other things your training at Luther College was very helpful to you, I would imagine, was it not?

Adm. H.: Oh, yes. As a consequence of that training and I suppose as a consequence of my own interests — I'd like to get this absolutely correct — I think that I stood one in

English in my class as a plebe every month but one. That was a direct consequence of my classical education at Luther and my own interest in reading.

With regard to the courses at the Naval Academy otherwise, if you're interested in my reactions –

Q: Yes.

Adm. H.: I naturally found that I was handicapped to a certain degree by the gaps in my math, but that was left behind as soon as the first review of algebra was completed and we went on to other courses in mathematics. I possibly suffered in my appreciation of mathematics on account of the gap all the way through, because I never stood high in maths during my first couple of years at the Academy when we had mathematics as a subject per se. Geometry and trigonometry gave me no trouble. I had had them at Luther and understood them pretty well, but I suppose I would be obliged to say that my aptitude for math was not of the highest. That's about the best characterization that I can put on it.

On the other hand, my preparation in the classics led more or less naturally to my standing very high in English and French.

Q: French was the required language?

Adm. H.: Well, I'd never had French in college but I presume my study of languages at Luther, including the reading of

Hustvedt #1 - 14

German, of Latin, of Greek, all contributed. I had a little handicap in math, I think, but no handicap elsewhere.

Q: I imagine you had one great asset in that you knew how to study?

Adm. H.: Yes, I think I did. I think I knew how to make use of my study periods.

Q: How did you react to the drills and the routine and the regimentation of life?

Adm. H.: The regimentation didn't bother me in the least. I was accustomed not to regimentation but to orders in my youth.

Q: And discipline?

Adm. H.: Discipline, yes. I think I pretty well knew how to study. I know that I was ready and willing to conform to regulations. They didn't irk me in the least.

Q: Were there summer cruises in those days?

Adm. H.: Oh, yes.

Q: Tell me about them.

Adm. H.: Let me tell you about my first cruise. My first cruise was in the brig Boxer - a hermaphrodite brig actually. The Boxer was a little ship that had been built for the Navy primarily for training purposes and I think in that respect she was rather an innovation because midshipmen, prior to the advent of the Boxer I think had gotten their training so far as sail is concerned in the small boats at the Naval Academy and in the Hartford, which was a full rigger. But during my plebe summer the Boxer became available for the first time and the new fourth class was taken to sea on Chesapeake Bay in four sections, and taken to sea for a week at a time.

On the Boxer we were really trained as far as the time permitted in being sailormen because our drills were entirely connected with making sail, shortening sail, furling, and that sort of thing, and we were at it more or less all day long for the week we were out. We learned during that week what it meant to swing a hammock, we learned what it meant to have a ration of water because we were given one stroke of the hand pump in our little tin basins for our toilet in the morning, apart from that we got no fresh water except what we could drink at the scuttle butt. I have sometimes joked since about my introduction to the sea in that in the space of a month I went from the farm to being captain of the foretop learning how to handle the reef earing.

I was actually captain of the foretop during my week in the Boxer. I suppose perhaps I looked a little huskier than some of my classmates! I was a well-grown boy of nineteen at that time.

Q: How large was your class?

Adm. H.: We graduated 173. I can remember that figure. I think the number that were credited with entering in my class was something like 245, but I remember distinctly that 173 were graduated.

Q: So you had one week's cruise at least for your plebe summer?

Adm. H.: Yes.

Q: And the rest of the summer was spent - ?

Adm. H.: The rest of the summer was right there at the Academy. The cruise didn't take us any farther to sea than to Solomon's! I remember that we went that far, and I think Solomons was the one place where we had anything that approached liberty. It wasn't a liberty it was just a chance to stretch our legs ashore for an afternoon.

Q: Tell me about the following cruises, the much more elaborate cruises.

Adm. H.: Well, my first real cruise was what we used to call youngster cruise, which came between plebe and youngster years, and that was you might say a humdinger for the time, because for the first time in quite a while, I believe, we saw some foreign ports. I was assigned for that cruise to the Des Moines, which was a so-called protected cruiser of that era.

Q: "Protected cruiser," what does that indicate?

Adm. H.: That means she had a certain amount of armor here and there.

The captain of the Des Moines at that time was Captain Halsey, Bill Halsey's father, who was highly respected by all of us, apart from the fact that he was our skipper. The executive officer was named Cooper. I could practically give you the roster of officers there, but I might miss one or more so I think I'd better let that lie. The highlight of that cruise was that we sailed from Annapolis directly for Funchal, Madeira, and that was the first approach to a foreign cruise that midshipmen had in some years, I believe.

Q: What a delightful port to choose!

Adm. H.: Yes, Funchal is a wonderful place. Have you been there?

Q: Yes.

Adm. H.: Funchal was my first foreign port. I was there again on a cruise in the Bergensfjord three or four years ago and I found Funchal unchanged in some respects but very greatly changed in others. When we were there as midshipmen, the ship was constantly surrounded by small shore boats in which there were small boys who were constantly shouting "heave I dive, heave I dive, heave five cents in the water, small boy my brother, he dive." We had them all day long - "heave, I dive!"

I needn't describe Funchal. Of course, Funchal is exotic even now.

Q: Where else did you go?

Adm. H.: Our next port was Horta in the Azores. Have you been to Horta?

Q: I've been to the Azores but not to Horta.

Adm. H.: Horta is not frequently visited, I think, but it was interesting. I remember getting ashore there once and taking a longish walk, seeing what the countryside looked like. Of course, Horta was a very small place in those days. Interesting, of course, at Horta was the fact that from there we could see Pico, the volcanic island of the Azores. It was a piece of our landscape there at Horta because Pico was very distinctly in sight from Horta.

Oh, incidentally, I think I have not mentioned that between Chesapeake Bay and Funchal we had heavy weather practically all the way, and I mean heavy. Nearly all the midshipmen were out of commission. I can remember one supper when the midshipmen's mess had gotten down to the point of swinging one table. The tables in those days were hung from the hammock billets, and they swung. Swinging one table and putting food on the table and letting the midshipmen grab what they could as it swung, and I think there were not more than half a dozen of us at the meal at that particular time.

Q: I take it, then, that you neglected the coaling of the ship?

Adm. H.: Coaling, of course, we participated in. We participated in it during all our summer cruises. I happened to be assigned to the lookout detail during the first week of that cruise, and the lookout detail — I think it was a watch in four — but the lookout actually made his way to the crow's nest on the foremast and that's where he stood his lookout watch. I think that I was the only one on that lookout detail that wasn't actively seasick at some time or other. So my introduction to going to sea was pretty rugged there in the Des Moines and convinced me that I need never worry about being seasick.

Q: Did it help convince you that you really wanted to be a sailor?

Adm. H.: Well, it helped to convince me that seasickness was never going to be one of the handicaps!.

Q: This cruise didn't take you to the continent of Europe?

Adm. H.: No, not at all, and I don't remember any particular grousing about it, but I do remember my own feeling of disappointment that we should have crossed the Atlantic and merely seen Funchal and Horta, because you're almost across the Atlantic when you get to Madeira and the Azores, as you know.

Q: Yes, but this was Columbus's route, wasn't it?

Adm. H.: Almost. I would say almost the reverse of Columbus. From the Azores we came back to the coast of Maine, Bar Harbor. I don't think we went to Bath on that cruise. We went to Bar Harbor, which of course is very interesting, and I think from Bar Harbor to Boston. At Boston on a Sunday I saw my first big league baseball game, and one of my recollections of Boston at that time was seeing one of the first large electric advertising signs I'd ever seen and it advertised Buick! Automobiles weren't very numerous in those days.

Q: No.

Adm. H.: Then, from Boston we went to Newport and New London and then went on back to Chesapeake Bay and our home port of Annapolis.

Q: Were you required to do any formal studying while you were on the cruiser?

Adm. H.: No.

Q: You didn't have any of the professors with you?

Adm. H.: I'm sure we did not on the Des Moines on my youngster cruise. We did on the Olympia on my first class cruise.

My class didn't take a second class cruise I think the reason for that was that the Navy Department was finding it difficult to scrape up suitable ships at that time. That was the year of the Exposition at Hampton Roads and a good deal of what the Navy had available that summer in addition to the active fleet I think went into Exposition matters.

Q: So what did you do with your summer?

Adm. H.: Well, the new second class was divided into two sections that summer, and one section went on leave while the other section stayed at the Academy and more or less participated in the indoctrination of the new plebe class, in addition to having our own exercises. So we had two months' leave that summer and two months at the Academy, in two different sections.

Q: Did you go home on your leave? Did you go back to Chicago?

Adm. H.: Yes, I went home to Decorah, Iowa on that leave and also on the other, what we used to call September leave, I guess they still do. I think I haven't mentioned that my plebe summer I became one of what was known as the typhoid squad. Have you ever heard of that typhoid epidemic?

Q: No. Tell me about that.

Adm. H.: Well, that was the summer of 1905 and, as I remember it, the typhoid began in late July and I was one of the plebes who were taken with it about the middle of August. I was in the sick bay for about a month and then sent on leave for about a month to recuperate. The upper classmen, I think, were given an extra week of September leave on account of that typhoid epidemic, and I myself got back to the Academy about the middle of October. In the meantime I had missed half the summer of instruction in French and I think about a month or more of instruction in mechanical drawing. I didn't know how to fill a rightline pen when I came back from that leave, and my classmates already had a month or more of mechanical drawing under their belts. The consequence of that was that I was almost unsatisfactory in mechanical drawing for several months.

Q: Were many of the boys afflicted with typhoid?

Adm. H.: Not more than, I would say, somewhere in between six and ten. I remember that there were one or two - two I think, who on account of their timing or on account of the severity of their cases missed so much of the academic year that they were forthwith turned back into the next class, told to go home and come back next June. Luckily I escaped that.

Q: Was there a typhoid carrier there, or how did it originate?

Adm. H.: My own guess is that it originated through our having swimming lessons off the Santee wharf after we had qualified in the little indoor pool. Swimming was on the schedule as a regular drill and after a plebe qualified in the little pool he joined the swimmers and he swan off the Santee wharf. That was a summer of typhoid epidemics pretty well around the country, at least in the East. I remember there was a very serious one at Jamestown, New York, that summer, and there were various places where typhoid was rampant in that summer of 1905.

Incidentally, there was a certain amount of typhoid the following summer and several cases at the Academy, including one of the Japanese midshipmen, who died in the summer of 1906.

Q: Tell me about the first class cruise, the Olympia.

Adm. H.: It was entirely what we used to call a crab cruise. In other words, up the East Coast and back down again. I don't remember thoroughly in just what order we took our ports during that first class cruise, but New London, of course, was always one of the summer cruise stops.

Q: That was to visit the submarine base?

Adm. H.: Not primarily in those days. The submarine base at New London was actually a later development than that. I'm not even certain that we had submarines based in New London in those days. Some of the early submarines were based in Annapolis. My memory is a little hazy there, but I do not remember a submarine base at New London in the summer of 1908.

That summer cruise I don't think included Bar Harbor but it included Bath, Maine, where we took part in some kind of centennial celebration. I don't remember whether it was a bicentennial or more, probably not more than a bicentennial. We visited shipyards. We visited the shipyard at Fall River, as I remember, and of course the Bath Iron Works was going fairly strong at that time.

We spent a considerable time in the bays at the east end of Long Island, Gardiner's Bay and that area.

Q: What would be the purpose of that?

Adm. H.: An exercise area where we could man the boats, row, and sail, and so on.

I remember that that summer of 1908 was the first one that I can remember when motorboats began to proliferate.

Q: In Long Island Sound or where?

Adm. H.: No, not in Long Island Sound, in the ports like New London, for instance, and Bath.

Q: After this cruise, the last cruise, had you pretty much decided what direction you were going to take in the Navy?

Adm. H.: Well, of course, I presumed that I was headed for being a line officer. I hadn't developed any strong inclination or special aptitude toward engineering. Of course, at that time, the old Engineer Corps in the Navy was fading out and, as midshipmen, we didn't necessarily look forward to a choice between line duty and engineering duty. We were all going to be line officers, as far as we knew. Some might develop special aptitudes as engineers. Of course, in our summer cruises when we were on ships with engineering plants we stood engineering watches in our turn.

Q: What about ordnance, did that interest you?

Adm. H.: Not as a specialty. I afterwards had a postgraduate course in ordnance, but that was in later years.

Q: Tell me about your first assignment, then. Were you commissioned immediately upon graduation?

Adm. H.: We were the last class that served a full two years as passed midshipmen and, as a consequence, I think it's fair to say that we have rather suffered ever since in promotion, relatively. And in the matter of promotions, I think it's rather an irony that it even extended to the wartime promotions that came along in World War II.

Q: Oh, really. They were affected by that?

Adm. H.: Well, in this respect, that World War II brought about a flood of promotions, naturally. My class was the last class to undergo a selection process prior to World War II. As a matter of fact, I was the last individual to be selected for flag rank up to World War II, I was the last one.

Q: That's an interesting point.

Adm. H.: I was selected in the summer of 1941 and I was the last one on the list.

Q: When you graduated you went on the West Virginia as your first assignment. Tell me about that.

Adm. H.: The West Virginia was one of the class of armored cruisers that was built around the thrn of the century. There were about a dozen of them built, and they were regarded as capital ships and were named after states. The West Virginia was one of them. She was the flagship of, I think it was called, the Second Division of the Armored Cruiser Squadron, which was doing duty in the Pacific at the time I was graduated.

On the West Virginia my first duty was as assistant navigator, and during the first year that I was aboard and while I was assistant navigator we made a cruise from the West Coast to the Orient, which of course was a very interesting thing for us. We spent about a month in Hawaii on the way, not in port because we did a certain amount of exercise at sea during that month. One very interesting feature of that cruise to the Orient was that after we left Hawaii our first stop, which was a refueling stop, was in the Admiralty Islands. The

Admiralty Islands in those days were just one remove from savagery.

The anchorage that we used was in Naries Harbor, which is a very fine harbor several miles off the north coast of the main Admiralty island and is a harbor that was used during World War II as one of the steppingstones in moving from the Solomons on up through the Marianas and Carolines, the Marshalls, and all of those island groups. The base at Naries Harbor was used during that advance and certainly was far different then from what it was when I first visited there in 1909.

In 1909 the only inhabitants other than savages in that immediate vicinity, as far as I know, were a German trader who had a small establishment where he dealt with the natives largely for coconuts, I think. The natives, the men, dressed with only a g-string plus armlets, anklets, but they were pipe-smokers and carried their tobacco or whatever it was they smoked in gourds, stuck their pipes when they were not in use through their armlets, and were thoroughly savage.

I was detailed as a member of a survey party. EAch of the ships sent out a boat to run a boat survey there in Naries Harbor, which is a considerable expanse of water with a number of islands in it,

Q: Was this for the Hydrographic Office?

Adm. H.: Yes, that was for the purpose of developing the area more than the issued charts of that time because the issued charts of that time were rather sketchy down in that part of the world.

Q: So you may have contributed to the Navy's effort in World War II at that particular moment?

Adm. H.: As it so happened, when I left the fleet out in the Pacific in 1944 with orders to Washington for assignment to another command, my route led through Nariés Harbor in the Admiralty Islands. I actually left the ship almost up in the Marianas area - the name of the particular atoll escapes me now - and I went by plane from there to Pearl Harbor by way of the Admiralties and I landed by plane in the Admiralties and was held there over a Sunday. I got in there on Saturday and was held over Sunday and left on Monday morning. During the Sunday I was asked whether I would like to go with a boat that was visiting one of the temporary outfits ashore, which happened to be a radio outfit, on one of the islets. Well, I accepted that with great pleasure and I found that I was visiting the islet where, during my midshipman days, we had made a boat survey of Naries Harbor, the very islet where we had stopped to anchor and have our luncheon during those boat survey days. So I was landed almost exactly on the place where I had landed in 1909, but the appearance of the natives was a little different. They had become a little bit civilized in the close to forty years.

Everything else was just as it had been forty years before.

Incidentally, when we first started on that boat survey, the boat that I was in, which of course was the boat from my ship the West Virginia, cruised along the shore of one of the islets there looking for a place that would serve as an anchorage, which we found, but before we got to it we had attracted a flock of native men who came down to the shore as close as they could get to us. We were easing along at, I suppose, somewhere around 6 or 8, maybe 10, knots, looking, and all of a sudden this group of natives let go with a flock of spears! It was only a gesture, but it didn't look very inviting at the time. Their range, I think, was about halfway out to our boat, so it was only a gesture of some sort. But after we landed in the little inlet that we used as a base from there on, the natives swam out, came out in their little boats, and gathered around at a respectful distance. Of course, we couldn't communicate with them, except by signs.

We chose to anchor there for our luncheon and a considerable part of our luncheon was a big can of corned beef that had to be opened with a key. It was a big can and the key was about that long. Well, when we departed we left whatever there was in the way of scraps, including the can and the key and the rest of it. When we anchored there for our luncheon the next day, one of the first of the natives we caught sight of had taken the skewer out of his nose and was wearing that corned beef key through his nose! I suppose he was the dandy of the neighborhood, with an iron spike in his nose instead of a wooden one!

Well, we're straying.

Q: Did the Navy maintain units of the fleet in the Far East in those days? Or were these just voyages out?

Adm. H.: Yes, there was a Pacific Fleet in those days, but I doubt whether they ever got down to the Admiralty Islands. That's a far cry from Manila or Hong Kong or Shanghai or Yokohama.

Well, we went on from the Admiralty Islands to Manila and were in the Philippines for several weeks. I remember one circumstance of our stay there at Manila. We saw a ship depart from Manila for the West Coast that was carrying the first load of duty-free Philippine cigars to the U.S., and that was quite an occasion. It made a great deal of difference, I believe, to the economy of the Philippines actually, to be able to ship cigars to the States without paying duty on them. I remember seeing that.

A good part of our stay in the Philippines was at Olongapo, Subic Bay, where we based for docking in the old floating dry dock Dewey, which was based at Olongopo in those days, and we also got ready for and fired a long-range battle practice there. From the Philippines the fleet broke up into pairs - there were eight of us armored cruisers, they broke up into pairs for visiting ports. The ship that I was on, the West Virginia of that day, went to Hong Kong. The West Virginia and Pennsylvania were paired, as I remember it, and we went to Hong Kong.

Q: To show the flag?

Adm. H.: Yes, and to give liberty, I suppose, after having been out of civilization for a month or so. We were in Hong Kong I think for about ten days, maybe two weeks. There are a couple of things I remember about Hong Kong in addition to the things that any tourist visitor will see in Hong Kong.

One was the fact that there was a pair of German cruisers there at the time we were there and they were the Scharnhorst and the Gneisenau.

Q: Oh, really, of that day!

Adm. H.: Of that day. We exchanged visits of courtesy with the Germans. Of course, the topsiders had their official exchange of calls, but I remember that we had a wardroom calling committee that called on the Germans and they came and called on us. Those were days when even the junior officers had a wine mess, you know.

Another thing that was a landmark to me in Hong Kong was that I had an opportunity to visit Canton, to take a night boat up the river, spend a day in Canton, and take the night boat back. Canton in those days was a very interesting experience, of course.

Well, we moved on from Hong Kong to Nagasaki, incidentally encountering the tail end of a typhoon on the way with very heavy weather. I don't remember anything very special about that passage to Nagasaki, except that I do remember during the heavy weather relieving my immediate predecessor as junior officer of the deck, who was Richmond K. Turner, afterwards known in the South Pacific as "Terrible Turner"! You're familiar with Terrible Turner and Howling Mad Smith, of course?

Q: Oh, yes. Kelly Turner.

Adm. H.: Kelly Turner. I relieved Kelly Turner on the bridge on an afternoon that I remember very distinctly in that heavy weather.

Q: I'd like to ask you about weather forecasting in the fleet in those days?

Adm. H.: I don't remember any such thing as a fleet meteorologist or a fleet forecasting group of any kind, and, of course, radio communication was just in its infancy at that time. We had radio in the armored cruisers, but I don't remember that there was any system of weather forecasting or communicating weather forecasts by radio in those days.

Q: So you weren't forewarned about the typhoon, were you?

You just came upon it?

Adm. H.: As far as I know. Of course, we had whatever knowledge of weather we had acquired in the law of storms, but we had nothing like radio forecasts, I'm quite sure. I think radio was too much in its infancy at that time to have developed a network of radio forecasts. Radio was pretty new in 1909. I think I can remember that even the roentgen ray became known in the early 1890s, at least it came to my consciousness in the early 90s. I had never heard of such a thing as an x ray until I was, perhaps, 10 years old. Roentgen had been making his experiments and discoveries possibly before the 90s but I think the x ray came to popular attention actually about the mid90s, and radio communication later than that.

Q: Was the West Virginia joining units of the fleet out there? Did we have an admiral out there in the Far East?

Adm. H.: In the armored cruisers of that day we had two admirals. There were two divisions. I can't recall for certain, but I think not - I don't think there was a commander-in-chief, Pacific Fleet, at that time. I think there was a commander-in-chief, Asiatic, but I don't think there was a commander-in-chief, Pacific Fleet.

Q: Had you gone out, then, to join the Asiatic Fleet?

Adm. H.: No, we were making a swing. I think you might

say we were probably showing the flag in the Orient because we visited Manila as a fleet, we were at Olongopo as a fleet. Then we broke up into pairs, which would be four pairs. One pair, the one I was in, went to Hong Kong, Nagasaki, Tokyo Bay, Yokohama for Tokyo. One went to Shanghai. I've forgotten exactly where the Christmas holidays came in. I think they found us all in Tokyo Bay, but in the meantime ships in pairs had visited different ports in the China-Japan area.

Hong Kong, of course, was very much an international port in those days, more so than Nagasaki. Nagasaki was, of course, a much-used port of call but not nearly as international in those days as Hong Kong or Shanghai.

In Tokyo Bay, Yokohama, we were able to run up to Tokyo by rail for a day's visit.

Q: How were you received by the Japanese Navy?

Adm. H.: I don't remember anything much in the way of communication. I suppose there must have been official calls. I don't recall anything about that stop in Yokohama, except that there was a football game at one of the lovely parks in Yokohama between teams from the West Virginia and Pennsylvania. I don't remember whether that was a New Year's Day game or something of that sort. I think it possibly was on New Year's Day. Incidentally, the Pennsylvania won that game I think 6 to 0 over the West Virginia team, which was coached by me.

As you can imagine, there hadn't been much time for any organization of practice during our visits to the Admiralty Islands and the Philippines, and so on and so forth. This football game was pulled off more for the purpose of just having a game because I think the only practices that we could get in were during our stay of ten days or so in Nagasaki.

Q: How important were athletics to the fleet units at that time?

Adm. H.: There was a great deal of interest in athletics, particularly in boat racing and the fleet baseball encounters in the Pacific Fleet of that time. They really were of great interest to the men in the crews. The baseball games used to attract crowds, mostly of the ships' personnel, of course, the two ships that were engaged.

Well, we were at Yokohama for Christmas and visited Tokyo, and then we headed back home. We stopped in Hawaii just long enough to refuel, as I remember it, probably not more than four or five days, and then on back home on the West Coast.

Q: Let me ask what were the facilities in the Hawaiian Islands at that time?

Adm. H.: There was a coaling station. There was a naval station in Hawaii at that time. The facilities didn't amount to very much. There was access to a marine railway and there was coal. I don't suppose that oil was really a factor because none of us burned oil. Pearl Harbor had not been developed.

Q: Were there any repair facilities?

Adm. H.: Well, as I say, there was a marine railway that I think in those days could accommodate a destroyer. The iron works I think must have been keeping a certain amount of capacity for repairing ships because they had a great many steamships coming in to Honolulu in those days. Pearl Harbor, at that time, was undeveloped.

Back on the West Coast we went about our usual business. Of course, we were in those days having a schedule of target practices, both short range and long range, and night. One of the notable events that some of us took part in as witnesses - the West Virginia, to which I was attached, and the Pennsylvania, plus I think other ships of the armored cruiser squadron, though I can't recall how many, were in San Francisco Harbor when Eugene Ely made the first landing of an airplane aboard a ship. I needn't go into describing that because that has been covered very fully here and there, but the West Virginia was anchored within 500 yards of the Pennsylvania, on which the landing took place, so, of course, we on the West Virginia in effect had grandstand seats for that event. I won't attempt to describe it. As I say, it's well known, the techniques that were used for arresting, the runway, but I don't remember seeing it mentioned, or, at least, stressed is that when Ely took off from the _Pennsylvania_ on that day his wheels, his landing gear, almost touched the water before he was airborne. It was a very, very close thing, his getting off for his return flight instead of splashing.

Q: What about the landing itself, that must have been a hair-raiser, too?

Adm. H.: It was done so quickly. He came in from a field south of San Francisco, flying at about 1,000 or 1,200 feet, and he went on up over the ships of the fleet that were anchored near the San Francisco landing and on up to the neighborhood of Goat Island, where he turned around and came back down. During that return he was losing altitude and he came down past the ships again until he was at a fairly low altitude off south San Francisco, somewhere in the Hunter's Point area perhaps, when he turned and came up fairly low and approached his landing. All I can say is that he made what we're all accustomed to seeing as a normal loss of altitude and the touch-down, except that he touched down on the platform, and of course the crude arresting gear did what was hoped for and stopped him before he hit anything except the deck. But taking off he had an awfully short run in the space of the distance between the mother cruiser's mainmast and and her stern. That's a run of certainly not more than a couple of hundred feet. And his drop-off at the deck I suppose was of the order of 15 feet or so, and his wheels almost touched the water before he was up to speed enough to be really airborne. It was a very thrilling thing to see.

Q: Did aviation at that point intrigue you?

Adm. H.: Not actively, no. I've never had any particular pull toward aviation. I have taken the controls of a plane, a dual-control plane, a few times on flights between here and Dahlgren, Virginia, flights when I was going down to Dahlgren in connection with ordnance tests when I was with the Bureau of Ordnance. I sometimes went down by plane and the plane would normally be a two-seater seaplane supplied by Naval Air Station, Anacostia. On one of those flights after I'd been with that particular pilot back and forth to Dahlgren several times, he took off from Anacostia one time and went up to about 1,000 feet, leveled off, and about the time he passed Mount Vernon he gave me a nudge and he took both hands off the controls. Well, I'd been around often enough to know what he meant by that so I took over the controls and I flew the plane, roughly from Mount Vernon down to Dahlgren. He took over as we approached Dahlgren and landed the plane - it was a seaplane - and the proving ground people had a boat out there to fetch us ashore and no sooner had we stepped ashore than one of the officers attached to the proving ground said to us, "Who was at the controls when you came around Mathias Point?" I said, proudly, I was." He said, "I knew it."!

Q: An amateur up there!

Well, going back to the West Virginia, your tour brought you back to San Francisco Bay, and then what?

Adm. H.: That landing on the Pennsylvania by Eugene Ely was within a matter of weeks after we got back to the West Coast and the next thing I can remember particularly about my days in the armored cruiser squadron on the West Coast was the fact that I was still attached when my examinations for ensign came up in the spring of 1911. I'm a passed midshipman all this time, you understand. But before those examinations came up the armored cruisers of the Pacific Fleet were ordered to base on San Diego. That was because of the fact that the Revolution in Mexico was still going on at a lively pace and there were revolutionaries as close to us as the city of Tijuana. As a matter of fact, during the period that we were based on San Diego there was a battle of sorts at Tijuana between government forces and insurgents and we happened to be aware in the fleet that we had certain men who had become absent without leave, some of them perhaps even become deserters, technically, who had joined the insurgents down in Tijuana.

Well, an engagement of sorts took place at Tijuana that spring and the government forces took possession of Tijuana and they also took some prisoners, and an arrangement was made for officers from individual units of the fleet to go down there in a group at an appointed time to see whether any of these prisoners could be identified as being over leave from ships of the fleet. I was designated to represent the West Virginia in that little expedition because I knew the crew pretty well, having by that time been on the ship nearly two years and having done a great deal of duty as junior officer of the deck and officer of the deck and checked in liberty parties and so on. So I knew the ship's crew pretty well. There were somewhere around 600 of them. So I was sent down to pick out the West Virginia's share of the prisoner crop, which I did.

Q: Had they gone as adventurers, or what?

Adm. H.: Oh, yes. Something to get a kick out of. But one of them, as it so happened, and he's the only one I remember as an individual, was a bo'sun's mate, first class, who was known throughout the fleet because he was the well-known coxswain of the West Virginia's race boat crew and was a character. He was an old-timer and he was a first class bo'sun's mate, I think only because he had a tendency to get into trouble and therefore couldn't hang on to the rating of chief - he would have been a chief otherwise, I think.

Anyhow, he was a first class bo'sun's mate and he was a Scandinavian. I don't know whether he was a Norwegian or a Dane, or even possibly a Swede, because his name was Huitfeldt. That could be a name from any of the Scandinavian countries, but it's more likely to be a Danish name I think than anything else.

Anyhow, he was known throughout the fleet, but he wasn't known as Huitfeldt, he was known as Vasco da Gama. That's the kind of character he was.

Q: Were these men incarcerated when you got them back?

Adm. H.: Oh, they were given courts martial and given punishment, probably loss of pay, and so forth.

Hustvedt #2 - 42

Interview No. 2 with Vice Admiral Olaf M. Hustvedt, U.S. Navy
(Retired)

Place: His residence in Washington, D.C.

Date: Thursday afternoon, 6 December 1973

Subject: Biography

By: John T. Mason, Jr.

Q: Last time, we got you back to the United States. Do you want to take up the story from that point, Sir?

Adm. H.: I believe I spoke before about the business of spending some months basing on Coronado and having recovered some of our deserters who had taken part in the Mexican revolution, didn't I?

Q: Yes, you did.

Adm. H.: Well, that takes us up to the time when I, together with my classmates, were taking our examinations for promotion to ensign. We were the last class to serve two full years as passed midshipmen.

Q: Was that a valid system, do you think?

Adm. H.: I don't suppose that it actually did us any particular harm because we performed the duties that ensigns performed afterwards, we were in the junior officers' mess, as the ensigns were afterwards, and I believe that after that on major ships ensigns were quite accustomed to standing watches as junior officers, junior officer of the deck and junior officer of the watch, in the engine room, and that sort of thing. I don't think that the status of passed midshipmen was far different from the status of ensigns in later years of comparable experience. Of course, I can't say that with absolute authority, never having been an ensign under those conditions. I had the experience of two years at sea after graduation before I became an ensign. But so far as my later observation is concerned I think as passed midshipmen we performed practically the same type of duty that ensigns of comparable length of service did later on, but we didn't have the rank and we didn't have the pay.

Q: And that is terribly important! That was just an aside. So, what was your next duty?

Adm. H.: My next duty after leaving the West Virginia was that I was ordered to the old cruiser Raleigh, which was a unit of the then Pacific Reserve Fleet. The Raleigh was a veteran of the Battle of Manila Bay, incidentally, and, of course, when I went to her in 1912 the Battle of Manila Bay was only fourteen years prior to that, so she wasn't so much of a superannuated veteran as you might suppose. That lasted with me for about six months, and it was a very quiet sort of thing because for most of the time we were moored in the harbor at Bremerton and we got under way only one time that I can remember - we got under way and proceeded to Seattle and took part in a civic annual celebration of those days which was known as the Potlatch. I think they have Potlatches to this day in Seattle.

In connection with that movement to Seattle we also went up the sound as far as Bellingham and stayed in Bellingham a few days before returning to Bremerton. In the late summer of that year, 1912, I was ordered to postgraduate instruction in ordnance.

Q: May I ask you a question first about the Raleigh? You say she was a part of the Reserve Fleet. Did they maintain a full crew on her as a reserve ship?

Adm. H.: No, she had a reduced crew and she had only five officers on board. The commanding officer was a senior lieutenant, there were two ensigns, and two warrant officers, one bo'sun and one machinist. That was the entire complement of officers, and the crew was a skeleton crew.

Q: But sufficient to take her down to -

Adm. H.: Oh, sufficient to get her under steam and to navigate her from Bremerton to Seattle and up to Bellingham and back again.

Q: Did the Navy have the practice of mothballing ships in those days?

Adm. H.: I think not, in the same sense that they mothball them nowadays. I think they were pretty well either in commission or in reduced commission, which was the category with our ships of the Pacific Reserve Fleet, or out of commission. I don't think we used the term "mothballing" at all.

Q: It was a kind of a limbo state that they were in - the Raleigh was in a limbo state?

Adm. H.: Not exactly because she was sufficiently manned and capable of getting under way. She was in reduced commission, you might say. I wouldn't call it "limbo" because she was able to operate and did operate to that extent during the six months I was on board.

Q: Yes. So you went to PG school?

Adm. H.: Yes. From there I went to postgraduate school as an ordnance student. My first assignment was to a one-year course largely in organic chemistry at George Washington University. This was supposed to be, for me, an introduction to becoming an "expert" in explosives, particularly in smokeless powders, but also in other explosives.

I was at the George Washington University for a year

and I was studying principally organic chemistry with a great deal of laboratory work.

Q: With the intention of getting a degree?

Adm. H.: Well, the degree was incidental to my year of postgraduate study there.

Q: I take it that the Navy at that point did not have a postgraduate school in Annapolis?

Adm. H.: The postgraduate school in Annapolis was just starting. Possibly you might say that it was in its first year. I think that so far as the ordnance postgraduates of that year were concerned, Fitzhugh Green and I were the only ones that were assigned to study in a civilian university. That's my recollection, but the postgraduate school at Annapolis had been started and it was based in the old Marine barracks across College Creek.

Q: Were there other ordnance men over there?

Adm. H.: The other ordnance men, as I recall it, were at Annapolis. I don't think any of them were assigned to study at a civilian college, other than Fitzhugh Green and myself.

Q: How did that happen?

Adm. H.: I wouldn't be able to explain it. I suppose they considered that the engineering postgraduates could be instructed at the Naval Academy. I know that in later years engineering postgraduate students were sent to universities or civilian colleges, but I don't think that had begun during the year that Fitzhugh Green and I were studying at George Washington. If it were so, I don't remember which of my classmates were assigned to colleges as students of engineering.

Q: As an ordnance man studying at George Washington University, you were also based at the Bureau of Ordnance?

Adm. H.: I was technically attached to the Bureau of Ordnance, yes.

Q: Did you have to report in there all the time?

Adm. H.: I didn't have to report regularly to the Bureau of Ordnance, no. I reported to the Chief of the Bureau when I first arrived in Washington for that duty, but after that I had no schedule of checking in at the Bureau of Ordnance.

Q: What was the caliber of the courses at George Washington?

Adm. H.: The courses that I was taking were under the Department of Chemistry, of course, and the head of the Department of Chemistry at that time was probably the foremost authority in the country, of the time, in the chemistry of explosives. He was Dr. Charles E. Monroe, who was not only the head of the Chemistry Department at George Washington University but I think was a Vice President of the

University, or had some collateral duty of that kind.

I think I'm safe in saying that Dr. Monroe at that time was the Number One expert in the country in the chemistry of explosives. That's why we were there.

Q: Yes. Did you select this area to pursue?

Adm. H.: No. I was assigned to that area. I had no special talent for chemistry. There were the two of us assigned, as I mentioned a few minutes ago. Fitzhugh Green later on and about the time we finished our courses at George Washington was ordered, I think through his own efforts, to duty with the North Polar Region Expedition that was starting, I think in 1913, under Donald McMillan.

Q: Well, Admiral, you spent two years in study at this point, did you not?

Adm. H.: Yes, but the second year was spent in studying on my own, so to speak, the operations of various industrial set-ups. First of all, after finishing my academic year at George Washington University, I was sent to the naval proving ground and powder factory at Indian Head, Maryland. Of course, that tied in directly with my having studied chemistry, particularly as related to explosives. The powder factory at Indian Head was the next natural stopping point. At Indian Head I had experience, not instruction because I was on my own practically, but opportunity to observe the manufacture of powder and also the operation of the proving ground itself, which at that time was located at Indian Head, Maryland, now at Dahlgren, Virginia.

I was as Indian Head from June until the following April, with a small interlude of about a month when I relieved the naval inspector of ordnance at the Washington Steel and Ordnance Company while he was given a month's leave.

After Indian Head I was sent to Pittsburg under the Naval Inspector of Ordnance at the Carnegie Steel Company, but I was there not so much to go into the manufacture of steel but spent most of my time at the Experimental Station of the Bureau of Mines, which was and I believe is located in Pittsburgh, and there, of course, I was primarily attached to the section of the Bureau of Mines' station which related to explosives used in mining.

After that period in Pittsburgh I moved on - oh, incidentally, while I was attached to the office in Pittsburgh I took my examinations for promotion to lieutenant, junior grade. From Pittsburgh I moved to the Philadelphia area where I was attached to the office of the inspector of ordnance at the Midvale Steel Company. Again, I was not concerned so much with the steel-making as I was concerned with the operations of the Army's Frankfort Arsenal, which had to do with small-arms explosives.

Q: This was what came later to be known as a Cook's Tour you were taking!

Adm. H.: While I was at Midvale I received my orders to sea, approximately upon completion of two years ashore, and was ordered to the USS Utah.

Q: Let me ask you a question about that tour of industry. Coming, as it did, on top of your year of intensive study at the University, this was in a sense implementation of what you learned in theory?

Adm. H.: Yes, I think it was intended to be, particularly of course the tour at the powder factory at Indian Head and also the tour connected with the Frankfort Arsenal, where the Army was dealing with explosives to a certain degree. Also while I was at Pittsburgh I performed inspections for the inspector at the Semple Company in Sewickley, which was manufacturing fuses and related equipment for the Navy at that time.

Q: So indeed this was a very valuable educational process you had?

Adm. H.: Yes, I was supposed to have a look at the application of explosives where they were manufactured or where they were applied to ordnance weapons.

Q: In retrospect, would you say that this was a great assistance to you in future years in your career?

Adm. H.: I would say that my study and observation and experience during those postgraduate years were of use to me in familiarizing me with the explosive and pyrotechnic elements that the Navy uses - smokeless powder, pyrotechnics, primer materials, smoke-producing materials, and that sort of thing. Quite a wide range when one considers all the various facilities to which I was attached during that second year when I was not having formal education of University lectures and study.

Does that answer the question?

Q: I think so, yes.

Now, you were about to tell me you had been assigned to the Utah.

Adm. H.: Yes, I was ordered to the Utah and there I became a turret officer, a division officer with a turret and its crew. I don't know that there was anything really out of the ordinary about my cruise in the Utah. My experience was pretty much that of any ensign aboard a battleship, I think.

Q: War had broken out in Europe by that time?

Adm. H.: The war broke out in Europe about a month before I went to the Utah.

Q: Did it have repercussions immediately in the fleet?

Adm. H.: I would not say that anything of that kind

impressed itself upon me. Of course, I was not in the fleet at the time the war broke in Europe, which was in August. I joined the Utah rather late in September, as I remember it, so there was no immediately observable repercussion in the fleet.

Q: Did you find any concern, any feeling that we might get involved in this conflict?

Adm. H.: I don't think I did in 1914, no. I don't think the country did in 1914.

Q: No, but military people sometimes are more sensitive to these things than others.

Adm. H.: Yes, but I'm afraid that as a young officer attached to a battleship and with family responsibilities because I had been married for two and a half years at the time World War I came on, I don't think we really forecast during the early years of 1914 and 1915 that we would be involved in Europe. I doubt that it occurred to us right away.

Q: The Utah operated in the Atlantic?

Adm. H.: The Utah operated entirely in the Atlantic during the years that I was in her, yes.

During my couple of years in the Utah I was transferred from command of a turret division to a function which at that time was, I believe, new to the fleet, that of assistant fire-control officer which, in effect, was assistant gunnery officer. The practice of having an assistant fire-control officer in a battleship I think was instituted somewhere about 1915 or 1916, and that's what I became in the Utah, assistant fire-control officer.

Q: The need for this function had become apparent?

Adm. H.: Yes. I think that was largely a result of the development that was taking place in what we call fire control. We were learning a certain amount of what the British were learning through their experience in the war in Europe beginning in 1914. By 1915 or 1916 we had learned to look upon gunnery, fleet gunnery, not only through the experience of our own service in prior years but also, in some degree, through the wartime experience of the British. Of course, that's a long story. The way it affected me was to switch me from a turret and division officer to that of assistant fire-control officer.

Q: I take it, then, the British were sharing some of their knowledge with us?

Adm. H.: Oh, yes. I couldn't say definitely, having been quite a young officer at that time, just what the extent of that sharing was nor what the channels were or the mechanics of sharing, but there is no doubt that we became acquainted with the developments in fire control and gunnery as a whole through the British experience of those years prior to our own entry.

Q: This new assignment must have added to your knowledge?

Adm. H.: Yes. Gunnery and fire control were very live topics in our fleet at that time. It was around that period that Admiral Sims made his presence felt, as we all know, in the improvement of naval gunnery. Gunnery was a very live topic in our fleet, there's no question about that, and to some extent, as I said, I think we shared the experience of the British even before we got into the war, just through what channels I wouldn't attempt to say because at the time I didn't know too much about it, being a relatively junior officer.

I was a lieutenant practically through World War I.

I was detached from the Utah in 1916 and ordered to the staff of the Division Commander, who was then Rear Admiral A. F. Fechteler.

Q: The father of William Fechteler?

Adm. H.: The father of Bill Fechteler, yes. I was ordered to his staff as flag secretary.

Q: He was battleships, too?

Adm. H.: Yes, he was the division commander of the division that I was in at the time in the Utah. The flagship at that time was the Florida but within a matter of weeks almost through a relative movement of organization Admiral Fechteler transferred his flag to the New York, which was in another division and, of course, was a more modern ship than the Utah. I was with Admiral Fechteler in the New York at the time we began to be closer and closer to a break with Germany.

At the time of the break with Germany I was still serving on Admiral Fechteler's staff and was just approaching my promotion to lieutenant commander.

Q: What was it like to serve as his flag secretary?

Adm. H.: Well, service as flag secretary is an education in the administration of the fleet. As flag secretary, it was my responsibility practically to prepare most of the correspondence related to official matters, schedules, et cetera. Of course, the Admiral indicated to me what he wanted but it was up to me to compose and phrase most of the correspondence and eventually present it to the Admiral for his signature, if he cared to sign it as was, or for amendment.

Q: All this done in longhand, too?

Adm. H.: Mostly, although I had two yeomen on my office staff who could take dictation, so a good bit of it was dictated. Some was in longhand before it was typed. Of course we had mimeographs in those days and methods of duplication but the text of important letters was often done in longhand by the Admiral himself or by me as flag secretary. Some of it was dictated. The Admiral used to dictate on occasion. I dictated on occasion. So it was some of this and some of that.

Q: A transitional time, wasn't it?

Adm. H.: I went to that duty in the spring of 1916 and in the spring of 1917 the war came on, and very shortly after that there was a shift in commands in the fleet. Admiral Fechteler was overdue for shore duty, as I remember it, and went to command at Norfolk. He was relieved by Rear-Admiral Thomas S. Rodgers, who was already a division commander in the fleet but by a certain amount of reorganization Admiral Rodgers came to be the division commander for whom I worked.

Q: And shortly thereafter you went to England, didn't you?

Adm. H.: No, it wasn't shortly exactly. I went with Admiral Rodgers I think in the early spring of 1917. I was with him from then on until late in 1918. I was still with Admiral Rodgers in 1918 when his division was sent overseas to join up with U.S. Naval Forces in Europe operating in conjunction with the Grand Fleet but not in company with the Grand Fleet. The Grand Fleet was based at Scapa, as it had been throughout the war. Battleship Division Seven with a somewhat reinforced division of destroyers was based on

Bantry Bay in Ireland.

Q: What were the particular duties of Division Seven?

Adm. H.: I think Division Seven was based on Bantry Bay as a counter to a possible sortie of German battle cruisers to raid our transport lanes. That's about as concisely as I can express my idea of what we were doing. Of course, Bantry Bay was within easy distance of the lanes that were used in ferrying our troops and materials to Europe, to the Western Front.

I recall that one time while we were there at Bantry Bay there was an alert of some kind which sent us out from Bantry Bay to meet with a troop convoy. Nothing out of the ordinary resulted from that. We picked up the convoy in pretty thick weather and escorted them to somewhere within the English Channel before we turned them over to local escort. That was the only time that we actually sortied from Bantry Bay in a war movement.

Q: The German submarine menace was particularly great in the North Atlantic at that point, was it not?

Adm. H.: Oh, yes. This was in the late summer and early fall of 1918. The submarines were very active and, of course, I presume that there was also always a chance that the Germans might spring loose one of their battle cruisers to raid the transport lanes in the Atlantic. I think that was in the background of the thinking too at that time, and that was the reason that we had this division of battleships at Bantry Bay, perhaps more to act as a counter to the battle cruiser menace than anything else. It was not primarily as a counter to the submarines because a battleship is a poor agent to hunt down submarines.

Q: Yes, indeed.

Adm. H.: We were still there when the armistice came on. Incidentally, there are two things that I probably should mention there.

During that time at Bantry Bay, in the early fall, late September, as I remember it, a deputation, for want of a better word, was sent from Admiral Rodgers' command to visit the American command operating with the British Grand Fleet out of Scapa. That was a sort of liaison visit so that Admiral Rodgers' command at Bantry Bay would be a little better informed about how things were done in the Grand Fleet with which he might join up at any time. That deputation consisted of Commander Ford Todd, then the executive officer of the *Utah*, of Gardner Caskey, who was the gunnery officer of the *Oklahoma*, of W. W. Wilson, who was the gunnery officer of the *Nevada*, and myself, who was still flag secretary to the admiral in command.

We proceeded by rail from Bantry Bay to Dublin, then across to Holyhead, in Wales, then by rail on to Crewe, where we waited for a night train to Edinburgh. We joined the Grand

Fleet just a day or so before the Fleet sortied from the Firth of Forth for one of its sweeps in the North Sea. Of course, the British battleships and our own battleship division there under Admiral Rodman were the last units to sortie from the Firth of Forth to form up outside and that led to our having a grandstand seat for the sortie. That was a most impressive sight, never to be forgotten.

We were at sea for three days or so and we made no landfalls, but I understood that we had come within ten miles or so of the southwest coast of Norway during that sweep. At the conclusion of the sweep the entire fleet wound up at Scapa Flow, in the Orkneys.

Q: That was a sortie, was it also a kind of a baiting operation, hoping that the German ships could be enticed out?

Adm. H.: We had that general understanding, that the Grand Fleet made an occasional sortie and sweep of that sort in the North Sea, largely in the hope that the Germans might be enticed. We understood that that was the case, yes.

Q: And you were disappointed!

Adm. H.: Yes! Well, we certainly had no such eventuality. But the weather, as I remember it, was somewhat thick during practically all of that particular sweep, but it was a very interesting thing, of course, to actually be at sea in the

North Sea with the British Home Fleet and our squadron with the possibility that a major action might be in the offing.

Our little group left the fleet within a very few days after arriving at Scapa and we took a train again down to London and reported in at Admiral Sims' headquarters in London to become acquainted with our opposite numbers there and to pick up whatever was appropriate in the way of indoctrination from Headquarters, London.

From there we took train again back to our base at Bantry Bay.

Q: You didn't look in on our submarine operations out of Queenstown?

Admm. H.: No, we really didn't touch Queenstown at all. The Queenstown command consisted primarily of submarines and destroyers and we had no primary hook-up with them. Our primary hook-up was with the battle fleet, which was a combined British and U.S. fleet up in Scotland.

Not long after we got back from that expedition, in a matter of weeks, I remember meeting Commander Caskey, then gunnery officer of the Oklahoma, and Commander Wilson, then gunnery officer of the Nevada, for a walk ashore on a Saturday or Sunday during which we climbed Hungry Hill, the principal "peak" in the area of Bantry Bay, and within a very few days after that Commander Caskey was stricken with 'flu and died within a couple of days. That autumn was a time of rampant 'flu epidemics both in Europe and in this country and we caught it at Bantry Bay.

Q: It took away a large number of your men, did it not?

Adm. H.: There were caskets being shipped out of our base at Bantry Bay daily for a matter of weeks.

Well, I went to the Oklahoma, 25th Gunnery Officer and I was in the Oklahoma when the armistice came on, which was not more than a matter of weeks later, possibly months -

Q: You personally escaped the 'flu, did you?

Adm. H.: Oh, yes, I didn't get it. As a matter of fact, I don't remember that we had it very severely in the Utah, which was our flagship at that time.

In any event, Commander Caskey's death left a vacancy in the Oklahoma for a gunnery officer and I was sent there, so from then on until the end of the war I was gunnery officer of the Oklahoma. The armistice came within a matter of weeks and within a matter of weeks after that we went to Brest - no, we went to Portland, Weymouth, in England for a brief liberty period, and then moved on to Brest and were in Brest when President Wilson came over for the first session of the peace conference-

Q: Let's go back for a second. What kind of a celebration did you have in the fleet at the time of the armistice?

Adm. H.: I don't remember an overt celebration, but there may have been some non-regulation ringing of the ships' bells or something of that sort. I don't think there was any sounding of whistles and sirens because I would suppose that, being anchored, we had no steam on the whistle and siren, unless it were authorized. I don't remember a celebration. I think we took it thankfully but quietly.

Q: And then that other point, the surrender of the German fleet. Were our units present for that?

Adm. H.: No, I don't remember just when that was. I suppose it was a matter of a very few weeks after the armistice, but we had no part in that.

Q: That was largely Royal Navy?

Adm. H.: Well, that took place in Scapa, and Scapa was a good long steaming distance from Bantry Bay in Ireland. No, we had no part in the surrender.

Q: Did the Oklahoma act as something of an honorary escort to the George Washington on that occasion when President Wilson came?

Adm. H.: Yes. It's my recollection that we met the George Washington at sea and escorted the President into Brest. In fact, I'm quite sure that we did. We must have left Portland-Weymouth and met the George Washington in the Channel somewhere. I know that we escorted the George Washington into Brest and that we then lay in Brest for possibly a week, and then joined, I think, by our ships from Scapa, we returned home and had a gala fleet review in New York the day after Christmas. Christmas Day we spent at anchor off the lightship.

Q: Busy polishing things up!

Adm. H.: Well, we weren't ashore for Christmas.

Q: How were you received in New York?

Adm. H.: Oh, there was a big to do in New York, a review going in and a parade on shore a day or so afterwards, but the holidays were impending then and I think after that initial reception we just settled down to having a stay in port in New York before going down to Guantanamo for the winter.

I had no particular celebration of my own. My family, which then consisted of my wife and two little girls, were with my people in Iowa. They'd been there since late summer, and I didn't see them until pretty close to a month later. Then I had leave incidental to being detached from the Oklahoma and ordered to shore duty in the Bureau of Ordnance.

Q: How natural that was, to get you back in the Bureau.

Adm. H.: Well, that led to my first real acquaintance with the Bureau because while I had been a student officer I was technically attached to the Bureau but I didn't see the Bureau except when I reported and was detached, as far as I can remember.

After the war I was ordered ashore to my first regular shore duty, you might say, apart from my postgraduate course, and I was ordered to the Bureau of Ordnance as chief of the experimental section.

Q: What did that entail?

Adm. H.: It entailed being officially in charge of the general experimental programs of the Bureau, which had to do largely, naturally, with ammunition, chemical warfare, if any. Experimental developments involving chemistry rather than metallurgy or mechanical applications et cetera.

Q: Here was the first real application of your postgraduate learning?

Adm. H.: The first real application to formal duties, and that was four years later.

Q: How interested was the Bureau in chemical warfare at that time, it having been practiced in World War I?

Adm. H.: We were never into chemical warfare in the sense of producing a gas weapon. We were interested in chemical warfare to the extent of experimental ammunition, of pyrotechnics, of smoke projectiles -

Q: Smoke screens?

Adm. H.: Yes, that sort of thing. Never any connection with lethal chemical weapons.

Q: That was largely the province of the Army, wasn't it, the lethal chemicals?

Adm. H.: Yes.

Q: How valuable were the lessons from World War I as they applied to smoke screens and that sort of thing?

Adm. H.: I don't remember that in the Navy we were tremendously interested in chemical smoke screens. Of course, we had had techniques in the Navy for many years for projecting smoke with oil as a fuel. We could lay down a smoke screen out of our smoke pipes at any time, burning oil. So I don't think the Navy was ever particularly interested in chemical smoke screens as such. WE were interested in smoke-producing projectiles, you might say, for the production of signals and also for the production of a surface screen to be laid by airplanes dropping what I think we called smoke bombs.

Q: Yes, smoke bombs.

Adm. H.: Which could be dropped from a plane and give off a chemical screen. We were interested in that sort of thing, but I don't think we saw any wide application for chemical smoke in the Navy.

Q: Did the Navy, Admiral - I'll preface this by saying I know that immediately following World War II a concerted effort was made in the Navy to collate the lessons learned during the war and then to begin to profit by that and to apply them - was the same thing done after World War I? Within your Bureau, did the Bureau of Ordnance attempt to assemble the lessons learned?

Adm. H.: Well, I think the answer would be yes. If you say did we assemble for formal symposiums and that sort of thing, I don't remember that we did. Is that an answer?

Q: Yes. After World WAr II they brought in officers who were assigned this specific task and spent a whole year, I suppose, preparing reports.

Adm. H.: At the time I joined the Bureau of Ordnance, which was a couple of months after the armistice of World War I, the Bureau was engaged in transforming itself from a war footing to a peace footing and, of course, trying to keep up projects which seemed suitable for continued development with reduced personnel, reduced funds, et cetera, et cetera. The experimental section of the Bureau of Ordnance, to which I fell heir in February of 1919, roughly three months after the armistice, had had during wartime officer personnel which I think amounted to six or eight. At the time I came there in February of 1919 the officer personnel was three, including myself, and as I remember it by summer it was one - I. There had been one officer attached to the experimental section who was a Reserve officer although he was a graduate of the Naval Academy and who was the one officer I had left after a few months, and presently I was faced with the necessity of getting along without him. Well, the upshot of that was that he qualified for employment as a civilian engineer and he stayed with me as a civilian engineer for a period of a few months. Well, to make a long story short of that thing, a laboratory was set up at the Gun Factory - the Naval Gun Factory in Washington -

Q: That was in the Navy Yard, wasn't it?

Adm. H.: In the Navy Yard, which was called the Experimental Ammunition Unit and that had technical personnel of, I think, initially three engineers. The one Reserve officer who had been my assistant in the experimental section of the Bureau was placed in charge of that unit as a civilian engineer, so that from then on I together with one clerk was the experimental section, Bureau of Ordnance. But I had a right arm, you might say, in the Experimental Ammunition Unit within the Naval Gun Factory at the Navy Yard.

Q: Yes, you had a working laboratory over there.

Adm. H.: Exactly.

Q: Did you have others? Did you have one down at Dahlgren?

Adm. H.: It didn't belong to me. Yes, there were ballisticians and that sort of thing at Dahlgren.

Q: What about Indian Head?

Adm. H.: Indian Head, of course, ever since it was established had had civilian chemists and chemical engineers et cetera, et cetera. Indian Head didn't belong to me. Dahlgren didn't belong to me.

Q: What were you concerned with primarily at that point in terms of experimentation?

Adm. H.: Such matters as experimental weapons and also such things as developments relating to new forms of ammunition primarily, new forms of pyrotechnics, new forms of fuses, et cetera, et cetera.

Incidentally, it's of interest to most people, I think, that among the projects, the experimental projects, that were in hand at the Bureau of Ordnance during the late years of the war was Dr. Robert Goddard's experiments with rockets.

Q: Indeed. Tell me what you know about that.

Adm. H.: Well, Dr. Goddard at that time was teaching at Clark University in Worcester, Mass., and he had begun, on his own, experiments with rockets as a means of propulsion. First, of course, as a means of attaining considerable altitude. I think that was what basically engaged Dr. Goddard's interest in it primarily, and during the war Dr. Goddard had entered into a personal service contract with the Bureau of Ordnance which supported his experiments through allotting him certain funds for materials and, at intervals, having him proceed from Worcester to Washington and to the proving ground at Indian Head for such experiments as he was ready to make.

During those periods he was on a per diem salary, you might say. At least, he was given a per diem pay, and that was the status when I came to the Bureau. That continued throughout my first tour of duty in charge of the experimental section of the Bureau. Dr. Goddard continued on that same basis. He worked on his own up in Worcester, I presume in his spare time because I think he continued to hold down his professorship at Clark University, but every now and then he would be ready for a little experiment at Indian Head. He would come down and visit the Bureau, consult with me, proceed to Indian Head, and stay there as long as he considered necessary to carry out the experiment that was on his agenda at the time.

Q: Did you go with him to Indian Head?

Adm. H.: No, not as a rule because if I had gone with him to Indian Head it would have been taking off a day from my desk and I was at that time the one officer on the desk.

Q: His experiments must have been intensely interesting to

you, however?

Adm. H.: Well, yes. Of course, we had no intention in the Bureau of Ordnance of supporting an investigation which would lead only to penetration of the upper atmosphere because that was outside of our purview. Our job was to provide the U.S. with weapons and protection against weapons. So Dr. Goddard's experiments had to have some possible application to naval warfare to justify our spending money on them in the Bureau of Ordnance.

Q: And that was his difficulty, was it not? I mean —

Adm. H.: Well, yes, he naturally to gain support from the government had to be able to hold out to the government a promise of a successful application for government purposes. Of course, the only government purposes foreseen at that time were military in character, because the government was not interested in pure science as far as the Navy Department was concerned, or as far as the War Department was concerned. The Bureau of Standards, maybe. But rocketry was being demonstrated with a view to possible application to weaponry.

Q: And it was considered rather esoteric, was it not?

Adm. H.: Yes, it was. There were many people, naturally, who at that time regarded Robert Goddard as a rather wild-eyed visionary. Well, nowadays we know what has resulted from Robert Goddard's visions, but at the time I'm speaking of, in the early 1920s, our interest was does this have some application to weapons.

Q: Is it practical!

Adm. H.: Well, we saw the possibility of certain applications to weapons, among them the possibility of extending our range for attack against submerged submarines. That was what was principally in our minds in the Bureau of Ordnance. Did this give us a chance of getting at submarines farther away than we do now, because at that time the range of attack against submarines was the antisubmarine depth charge to be projected from a so-called projector aboard destroyers –

Q: Catapulted off?

Adm. H.: No, not catapulted, propelled off with an explosive charge, but it had to be something that had a low order of recoil because destroyers can't stand the recoil of a tremendous weapon, and the depth charge, of course, including its arbor, which is what holds it until it's projected, weighs hundreds and hundreds of pounds. You can't project it except by what amounts to, in itself, a modified rocket effect from a depth-charge projector. A depth-charge projector is not a gun, it's really a double-barreled rocket, and it's double-barreled so that the thrust could have a counterthrust so as to reduce the actual thrust against the light structure of a destroyer.

So a rocket means of propelling a depth charge had certain theoretical attractions to it, and that's what the Bureau of Ordnance was really interested in in connection with Robert Goddard's experiments.

Q: How did you look upon him and his experiments?

Adm. H.: I felt that the rocket development was worthwhile and I was concerned with it and I supported it during the time I was chief of the experimental section of the Bureau from 1919 to 1922. Then I was ordered to sea.

Q: You had real rapport with Goddard, did you?

Adm. H.: To the extent that I had contact with him.

Q: What was he like as a man?

Adm. H.: Very shy, retiring, introspective I would say, probably. Most people regarded him as a visionary and I suppose to a certain degree he was a visionary. I don't think in the beginning that Dr. Goddard was at all interested in weaponry. I think he was interested in his visions of penetrating space. That's the idea I got from my contacts with him.

Anyhow, I went to sea in the late spring of 1922 and I was at sea then until early 1925 - January of 1925.

Q: Wait, now. While you were still in ordnance did you feel that you accomplished a great deal in that period there?

Did you advance the cause of ordnance by being involved with experimentation?

Adm. H.: Well, certain new projects certainly came along, yes.

Q: Were you somewhat curtailed by lack of funds? This was a time when the Navy was not expanding very much.

You smile!

Adm. H.: After the World War I situation was cleared up and the Navy went back on a peacetime basis, let's say, the naval appropriation under the Bureau of Ordnance carried a subhead called "experiments - ordnance." During those years that I'm referring to, the early 20s and the mid-20s, the subhead "experiments - ordnance" regularly ran to - don't laugh - $210,000 per annum. Of course, that was a token appropriation, you might say, and fortunately the business of experiments was not absolutely limited by that appropriation because the salaries of the people who were concerned, including my own and my civilian assistant and, later on, the two or three engineers in the Experimental Ammunition Unit, came out of a different appropriation. They didn't come out of that appropriation subhead. Also, there were certain materials that were accessible, that we could use, stock materials like powder and projectiles and certain chemicals out of stock, and that sort of thing. There were materials of that sort which were at hand in the Navy stockpile, so to speak, that could be applied to experimental purposes, insofar as they were suitable.

So the experiments that we managed to carry on were, you might say, largely paid for from sources outside of that small subhead "Experiments - Ordnance." And through perfectly legitimate means those materials and services were available without infraction of laws. But when it came to a thing like Dr. Goddard's personal services, that very distinctly came out of the little subhead "Experiments - Ordnance." There was nothing else to charge Dr. Goddard to because he was not a government employee and it wouldn't have been very practicable for us to ship such things as smokeless powder or what not up to him in Worcester. So Dr. Goddard's experiments were a charge against that infinitesimal appropriation subhead, you might say.

When I returned to the Bureau and to the same experimental section in January of 1925 I found that during my absence of two and a half years, all spent on sea duty in Hawaiian waters, that the personal service contract with Dr. Goddard had been terminated.

Q: He was too much of a luxury!

Adm. H.: Well, it was terminated because there was at that time no definite success in sight in applying the Goddard techniques to the propulsion of depth charges through the air. That was the long and short of that.

Q: Tell me, Sir, during that first long tour in the Bureau of Ordnance, tell me about your relations with the Army ordnance.

Adm. H.: We had perfectly open and cordial relations with Army ordnance through those years. We had an interservice committee, technical committee, which met at fairly frequent intervals to discuss matters of mutual interest in ordnance. I was a member of that committee, ex officio, when I was in charge of the experimental section, and so was my predecessor and my successor. My successor happened to be the same person as my predecessor.

Q: You played musical chairs in that job?

Adm. H.: Well, Theodore Wilkinson and I occupied that billet between us for something like, oh, pretty close to ten years, I guess.. No, it couldn't have been that long - somewhere around eight years, I suppose.

Q: I suppose in this first period, in the early 20s, there was no dream of such a thing as radar, was there?

Adm. H.: I think that during my period in the Bureau of Ordnance, which winds up in 1927, radar was still in laboratory and I think maybe treated as a rather confidential matter. I don't remember seeing radar in the fleet until about I would say 1937, 1938, 1939. I think during the time I was in the

Bureau of Ordnance, although radar may have been in the laboratory under the Bureau of Engineering, I don't think it had penetrated much farther and I don't remember it in the fleet until about 1938.

Hustvedt #3 - 77

Interview No. 3 with Vice Admiral Olaf M. Hustvedt, U.S. Navy
(Retired)

Place: His residence in Washington, D.C.

Date: Tuesday afternoon, 8 January 1974

Subject: Biography

By: John T. Mason, Jr.

Q: Well, Admiral, it's wonderful, as usual, to see you. I have been looking forward for some time now to a resumption of your story.

Today I think you're going to begin by telling me about your duty with Mine Squadron No. 2 with the Pacific Fleet, a duty you went to immediately after leaving the Bureau of Ordnance in 1922.

Adm. H.: Yes. You want some remarks on that service?

Q: Yes, indeed I do.

Adm. H.: Well, of course, that was my first command and the light minelayers of that time were converted destroyers so, in effect, it was a destroyer command of sorts. One drawback was that it was such detached duty, being based on Pearl Harbor, that I got very little fleet experience during that particular cruise, but a very enjoyable and, I have no doubt, very useful command experience.

Q: What largely were the duties?

Adm. H.: The Burns was a unit of the existing mine squadron of the Pacific Fleet, and she had an armament of mines. Our principal reason for being kept in training was to permit the laying of naval mines on short notice in waters that were strategically and tactically suited toward the use of anchored mines. We had no armament consisting of anything resembling a floating mine, they were all anchor-type mines, and from the very nature of the duties for which those vessels were equipped, the duty was largely separated from the operations of the fleet itself although we were a unit of the then Pacific Fleet.

Q: And the mines you used were World War I types?

Adm. H.: Yes, without very much modification. I think we were using the type of mine that had gone into the so-called North Sea Barrage of mines that was laid at the end of World War I -

Q: And which you were more intimately associated with, weren't you? You were rather intimately associated with them during World War I were you not?

Adm. H.: During the last months of World War I, I think I

have already recounted being attached to a flag command based on Bantry Bay, have I not?

Q: Yes, you have.

Adm. H.: I had nothing to do with mines or mining during World War I. My duty over there in World War I, as I think I've already recorded, was on the staff of the admiral commanding the detachment that was based on Bantry Bay and then succeeded to gunnery officer of the Oklahoma when the gunnery officer died in the 'flu epidemic in 1918.

Q: Well, reverting to the Pacific again, what were the facilities at Pearl Harbor at that point?

Adm. H.: You mean the general facilities?

Q: Yes, and as they pertained to minelaying.

Adm. H.: There was a mine depot at the Pearl Harbor station, and the mine depot and the minelayers of the squadron were the mine facilities. That's about what it amounted to.

The mines of our armament were kept on board, as far as that's concerned. The mine depot was there and available for supply, but by and large we had the mines on board at all times. Of course, that's not loaded. We dealt with dummy mines because in peacetime our function was to keep us prepared for the laying of live mines, but in our practice minelaying we were dealing with dummy mines. They were similar in all respects to the active mines except for not having any explosive charge.

Q: Were there any minesweeping exercises in conjunction with it?

Adm. H.: Yes. We had minesweeper types of that day, which were converted tugs, attached to the division. As a matter of fact, that little mine division was reduced in size at the time I joined it. It had consisted of an old cruiser type, the Baltimore, of that day as flagship and half a dozen minelayers, plus I think something like four sweepers. But about the time I joined, the Baltimore was put out of commission and the mine squadron was reduced actually to two minelayers and two sweepers. That's about what it amounted to during the time I was there.

Q: Wasn't it a period when personnel problems were great?

Adm. H.: Oh, yes, it was a time when the active ships were really being reduced pretty well around the whole perimeter, as I remember it.

Q: By contracting the fleet of minelayers were you able to maintain an adequate complement on board?

Adm. H.: Yes, ships' complements were not reduced.

Q: Was the submarine base at Pearl Harbor in operation?

Adm. H.: Oh, yes, the submarine base was in operation at that time.

Q: Was Nimitz there?

Adm. H.: No, I don't remember that he was there during any part of the time that I was in the mine squadron. It's my recollection that during the time I was in the mine squadron the ammunition depot where we stored our mines was under the command of Captain Leo Welsh.

Q: But the facilities were pretty limited in those days, were they not?

Adm. H.: Yes. Pearl Harbor was not, you might say, a developed fleet base at that time. I recall that during that period when I had command of the Burns the then Pacific Fleet made a cruise to Australia and, on the way, stopped in Hawaiian waters a while, I suppose a matter of a week or ten days perhaps. Admiral Coontz was the commander-in-chief at that time, and during that period my ship, the Burns, was detailed to take Admiral Coontz and a good part of his staff from Honolulu Harbor up through the Pearl Harbor entrance and into a berth at the base, whereupon they disembarked and visited the base and the base facilities, I presume the mine depot as well. Then I believe they were taken back to the flagship at Honolulu by automobile. I didn't have to return them to Honolulu. My job was done after I had embarked them in Honolulu and deposited them in a boat at the Pearl Harbor base.

Q: Did you have your family in Hawaii with you at that time?

Adm. H.: Yes, I had my family with me at that time. When we first got there, my wife's family, having been residents of Honolulu a good while, had a second home, you might say a summer home even though summer is prevalent in Hawaii the year round, had a vacation home, let's say, on the Pearl City peninsula. My parents-in-law were living there at the time so that, in effect, my family was going home to grandpa and grandma for a certain period, which was convenient and very pleasant. That didn't last throughout my tour in the Burns because Judge and Mrs. Cooper moved to California while we were still in Hawaii, and then we lived for a while at the peninsula place but eventually moved into town. Parenthetically, our elder son, Erling, was about two and a half when we went out there -

Q: That dates him, doesn't it! During leisurely moments did you have a chance to tour the other islands?

Adm. H.: No, not as a function of having leisure, but there were periods when we saw a great deal of the other islands because our real operating base for practices for mining and gun practices was Lahaina Roads, island of Maui, and our usual schedule was two weeks in the base at Pearl Harbor and a week operating from Lahaina. That was a fairly regular rotating schedule and during those periods at Lahaina we did our training under way, our practice laying of mines, and also fired our gun practices when they were due. So that Lahaina in a way was our practice operating base, while Pearl Harbor was the home base.

Q: Did the fleet in any sense use Midway in those days?

Adm. H.: Not that I can recall. We had nothing to do with Midway, but during the time that I was in command of the BUrns there was one expedition that we made to Johnston Island for the purpose of exploring Johnston and confirming or adding to the map and hydrographic information that the Navy had regarding Johnston.

Q: Was this at the behest of the Hydrographic Office?

Adm. H.: Yes, I think so. It was ordered by the Navy Department, I presume because the Hydrographic Office wanted to expand its knowledge and its information of what Johnston Island was like and what it offered perhaps in the way of potential base facilities.

There was during World War II a naval station of sorts at Johnston Island which I think serviced aircraft.

Q: You weren't thinking about those facilities in 1923!

Adm. H.: No, except that a part of the expedition to Johnston was I think a single seaplane - a single-seat plane - that did reconnoitering from the air and I think made landings in the lagoon, and that sort of thing. It was not a part of my command because the then-commander, I think, John Rodgers, actually flew the plane down there and he at that time, I think, was in command of the naval air units such as were then stationed at Pearl Harbor.

Q: Let's ask your son if he wants to ask a question about Pearl or anything of this sort.

Mr. H.: No, there's nothing I need ask now but of course you're in a period where I have direct experience. I remember this period well. I don't think I can add much at this point. If I'm around later on, perhaps I can.

Q: Well, you say this tour of duty gave you actual command experience?

Adm. H.: Yes, that was my first command experience.

Q: And that must have been an exciting sort of thing for you, was it not?

Adm. H.: Yes. Yes, of course, I suppose we all feel that we're ultimately being trained to command, and although that was not an independent command at all it had periods when I was acting on my own.

Mr. H.: If you want a sea story, you might ask for amplification on landing Admiral Coontz at Pearl Harbor.

Q: Yes.

Adm. H.: You're thinking of the way we made our landing at Pearl Harbor?

Mr. H.: Yes, that's a good story.

Adm. H.: The arrangement for taking Admiral Coontz and members of his staff from the flagship at Honolulu to the buoy at Pearl Harbor was made almost overnight, you might say, and was therefore somewhat sketchy. The way in which the transfer of Admiral Koontz and his staff from my command, the Burns, to the naval station at Pearl Harbor was like this. The normal berth of the Burns at Pearl Harbor was a buoy in what we called The Stream. In other words, it was a mooring buoy in the channel between the naval station at Pearl Harbor and Ford Island, where the aviation base was located. I was given no berth alongside the pier, so when the Burns made its way into Pearl Harbor she was bound, as far as I was concerned, to her normal berth at a buoy.

Q: And the Admiral could swim the rest of the way!

Adm. H.: No. As we approached that locality I saw that there was a launch standing by, which I assumed was there to take the Admiral and his staff ashore, but there was nothing to assist the Burns in securing at the buoy. So we just went through an impromptu performance as we approached the buoy, some of the members of the crew on the fo'c'sle had taken off their jumpers and their trousers and their shoes and socks, and as the ship was brought to a stop a few feet off the buoy, they simply dived over the side up in the eyes of the ship, swam to the buoy, and climbed on it and there they were to receive our lines.

That impromptu performance, I think, amused Admiral Coontz and his staff no end. I don't know whether they'd ever seen any landing quite like that, but it was the only type of performance that we could see on the Burns as being likely to get us secured to the buoy. So that's the way we did it! Of course, the boat then came alongside and took the Admiral and his staff ashore.

Q: Your efforts for Hydrographic, did they involve you with French Frigate Shoals in the opposite direction?

Adm. H.: No, we never visited French Frigate Shoals in my tour there, nor did we visit any of the outlying islands other than Johnston. There was a sort of annual liberty cruise in which we went to various of the established and recognized outlying ports in the islands. For instance, we went to Hilo at one time for a few days. We went to a couple of the ports on Maui, and we went to Kehului on Maui, at the time they had a Maui county fair, which made it a very interesting liberty port for all of us. But that was the extent of the cruising that we had in the Mine Squadron during my tour there of two and a half years.

There was a time when we wondered whether we could be taken along with the fleet on the fleet cruise to Australia, to which I've referred and which led to Admiral Koontz and his flagship being in Hawaii for a while. But that Australian cruise was not on our program.

Q: Why? Because your destroyer-minelayers were short-legged?

Adm. H.: I don't know that I ever heard any reason given for it, and I don't recall now just how much of the fleet made that Australian cruise - the battleships, of course, and there must have been some ships of the train that went there for supply purposes, perhaps independently.

Q: That was primarily a flag-showing episode?

Adm. H.: I think so and primarily a battleship operation, that's my recollection.

Q: Were you able to utilize any of your special ordnance knowledge while you were there on that tour?

Adm. H.: My specialized ordnance knowledge had to do with explosives, the chemistry of explosives, including primarily propellants, smokeless powder. I don't recall that my specialized knowledge of explosives ever came particularly into the picture during that period.

Mr. H.: He gave us a good show on the 4th of July with manual Roman candles!

Q: Oh, he did.

Adm. H.: That was a practical application!

Q: And a private one.

Adm. H.: I had forgotten that. That was at the peninsula, or was it uptown?

Mr. H.: I remember specifically up at Bibee house

Adm. H.: Oh. Well, there was a little public park across the street and I suppose that's where the Roman candles exhibition took place.

Mr. H.: I think you aimed them in that direction from our front walk.

Q: What were the school facilities like, for your family?

Adm. H.: School facilities existed but they were not located so as to be particularly available for my family. The two girls at that time - let's see, we went to Hawaii in -

Mr. H.: 1922 and they were seven and eight when we arrived.

Adm. H.: Yes, we went there in 1922 and our eldest child at that time was nine years old, the next one was about seven, and the next one was two and a half.

Q: His schooling was at home, was it not?

Adm. H.: Schools were not a great problem for the reason that when it came to teaching the two little girls my wife subscribed to the correspondence school in Baltimore, the Calvert School, and that turned out to be very satisfactory in every way, really, because of the flexible hours and of the excellence of the Calvert School courses and methods. We came to swear by Calvert School as a result of that experience, and I might mention that after we came back to Washington at the end of my cruise of two and a half years and put the little girls in public school, the elder one, who had been in school before we went to Hawaii, resumed in her regular place and we were told one time that the teacher of her class had said that there were two pupils in her class who stood out above the rest of them and they were so-and-so and so-and-so. One of them was our daughter. The other was the daughter of a Marine officer who had done a tour in Haiti, where that little girl had also been taught by Calvert School.

Q: In the home?

Adm. H.: In the home.

Q: And the home had a lot to do with it. I imagine that in your case your own thorough grounding educationally had some bearing on the situation.

Adm. H.: Well, of course, the fact that the Calvert School involves home instruction means, for one thing, that the pupil doesn't miss a lesson. Everything is thoroughly covered. My wife saw to that!

Mr. H.: I had two years of it myself, so I can attest to it.

Adm. H.: You had Calvert out there, didn't you?

Mr. H.: No, this was later. I did it in 1931-32.

Q: I think we would label him really precocious at the age of two and a half if he was doing this!

Well, Sir, after that very pleasant and profitable tour of duty, which it was, you came back again to Washington to the Bureau of Ordnance to the same berth?

Adm. H.: To the same section, yes, the experimental section.

Q: Was this something you wanted to do?

Adm. H.: Well, of course, I had realized from the time that I was assigned to postgraduate instruction in ordnance that my shore duty from then on for some time was almost certain to be a job connected with the Bureau of Ordnance.

Q: It was your destiny.

Adm. H.: Yes. I was tied to the Bureau of Ordnance for shore duty for a considerable period. I realized that.

Q: Did you find anything new under way in the experimental section when you came back?

Mr. H.: There were some things dropped that surprised you.

Adm. H.: I don't recall that there was anything revolutionary in the experimental program in the Bureau. The biggest change, perhaps, lay in the fact that aviation ordnance was changing faster than what you might call conventional gun ordnance. That's about the only thing I can think of.

Q: Did the Bureau of Ordnance work closely with the Bureau of Aeronautics at that point?

Adm. H.: Oh, yes, we had a close liaison with Aeronautics. The Bureau of Ordnance and the Bureau of Engineering both were closely tied up with Aeronautics.

Q: What was the attitude in the Bureau of Ordnance toward aeronautics and things that pertained to flight?

Adm. H.: Whether we worked in harmony and that sort of thing?

Q: Yes. Did you in the Bureau look upon it as a coming thing in the Navy?

Adm. H.: Oh, surely. I think that perhaps there has been a

great deal of misunderstanding, certainly at that time, of the attitude of the Navy toward aviation. I think the press of that time conceived the idea that because the Navy didn't fall in with the ideas of Billy Mitchell in regard to the development and administration of aviation, that the Navy was fighting air development, whereas, of course, the very opposite was true. It only needs to be pointed out, I think, that the first aircraft to cross the Atlantic was a Navy aircraft. But I don't think it's appropriate for me to go far into opening up any old controversy. I think it was undoubtedly the case in those days that the Navy was regarded to some extent by the press and public as being anti air development.

Q: I'm glad you make that point because that is a prevailing impression even now, I think.

Adm. H.: I can't imagine why. That is, I can't imagine why there is that impression nowadays. I think I know pretty well why it may have been the prevalent idea in those days, and the reason why it was a prevalent idea in those days was because General Mitchell was good for press copy any day. Of course, he was trying to do some things about aviation and with aviation that were certainly contrary to the interests of the Navy. The press had a nice controversy to oversee.

Q: The press always likes a controversy!

Adm. H.: Oh, yes. I think the Navy was to some extent cast in the role of being an opponent of air development, whereas I think the Navy was doing some wonderful things in the development at that time.

Q: The Navy had an exponent for air of unmatchable talent, and that was Admiral Moffett.

Adm. H.: Yes, Admiral Moffett was the head of naval air during the years that I was in the Bureau of Ordnance. I think during all the years that I was in the Bureau of Ordnance Admiral Moffett was head of the Bureau of Aeronautics-

Q: Did you have any personal contact with him?

Adm. H.: I don't remember any real personal contact with Admiral Moffett. Didn't you and I discuss the last time you were here something of the bombing tests against the ex-Germans? Didn't we cover that?

Q: Yes, but we didn't talk about Admiral Moffett. What were some of the developments in aeronautics that passed through your particular bailiwick in Ordnance?

Adm. H.: The Bureau of Ordnance had an aircraft armament section at that time which really took care of the supply of ordnance equipment to our air elements and also largely took care of the experimental aviation ordnance developments of the time like developing a bomb sight and that sort of thing.

The elements of ordnance for aircraft that came under my jurisdiction were largely related to explosives, pyrotechnics, propellants, powders, that type of thing, and not to such things as the actual supply of bombs, bomb sights, machineguns, and that sort of thing because the aircraft ordnance section was set up to look after that. The experimental section so far as aviation ordnance developments were concerned was secondary to the aviation ordnance section itself.

Q: Just as a matter of personal interest, was the Norden bomb sight being experimented with at that point?

Adm. H.: Oh, absolutely. Not only that but it was virtually perfected I think before the end of my direct connection with the Bureau of Ordnance. The Norden bombsight was either in actual production for our planes or was at the point of production.

Q: Did you know Carl Norden?

Adm. H.: Oh, yes, I knew Carl Norden very well.

Q: Did you have anything to do with the tests and experiments on the bombsight at Dahlgren?

Adm. H.: Yes. I was present for a good many of those tests.

I was not, as head of the experimental section in the Bureau of Ordnance, in charge because the aviation ordnance was in charge of that.

Q: You were something of an adjunct, though?

Adm. H.: Yes, and I had a great many contacts with Mr. Norden at that time in connection with other matters, although I was not administering his development of the bombsight.

Q: What other things did he work on in the field of ordnance?

Adm. H.: There was a time when a species of flying missile, you might say, or a flying bomb, so to speak, was an object of theoretical interest and it was in connection with that idea that most of my contacts with Mr. Norden took place. That plus the fact that during practically all of my second tour in the Bureau aviation ordnance and experimental ordnance shared an office room. Commander W. W. Wilson was in charge of the aviation ordnance section during most of that time and he and I had desks within a few feet of each other.

Q: Is that Gene Wilson?

Adm. H.: No, he was called Bill Wilson. Gene Wilson I think was never in the Bureau of Ordnance. He was in Aeronautics.

Q: Did the Norden idea of a so-called flying bomb sound feasible to Ordnance?

Adm. H.: Feasible enough to give some attention to the possibility. It never went very far as an actual development and tests.

Q: In retrospect, Sir, did his idea relate in any way to the kind of flying bomb the Germans produced in World War II, or the kind of flying bombs the Japanese produced?

Adm. H.: I would say that the general idea was probably almost identical, but I don't know whether any of the technical aspects were closely related. I can't really express an opinion on that because I don't know enough about what was done abroad, which, of course, was a good deal later than my time in the Bureau.

Q: Naturally, yes. I just wondered whether they were kindred ideas to the Norden idea of the 1920s.

Adm. H.: I presume that the underlying ideas were perhaps identical, a means of directing an effective explosive charge to a target at extreme distances. That's the basis of the thing, as I understand what you have in mind. Presumably, the basics were more or less the same, but we didn't go very far with that. I would suppose that one reason we didn't go very far with it was because the idea of mass destruction didn't make much appeal to us.

Q: Was the Bureau still involved with Dr. Goddard in this

second period when you were there?

Adm. H.: No, the Goddard contract had been allowed to lapse when I came back to the Bureau for the second tour, and as far as that circumstance is concerned I don't know too much about it because at the time the Goddard contract lapsed and when the discussions regarding it were going on, as they must have, I was in Hawaii.

Q: Was this a matter of real regret to you when you returned and found that the contract had lapsed?

Adm. H.: Yes, I was sorry to learn when I came back in 1924 that the Goddard contract was no longer in effect, but I didn't at that time figure that I could do anything about it. It was something that had been pursued for the Bureau's own purposes for a period of years, although not actively except on the part of Dr. Goddard himself. He was the active force, really, in those experiments.

I think, in considering that aspect of the Goddard story, it's well to consider that the actual product of the Goddard experiments even in those days, the actual end product, is exploration of outer space and the Bureau of Ordnance at that time did not have the mission nor the funds to develop the exploration of outer space. So I think the fact that the Bureau of Ordnance dropped the Goddard experiments back there in the 20s was logical enough from BuOrd's point of view.

Q: You say they did not have the funds to deal with that?

Adm. H.: No. Our funds were limited.

Q: Let me ask, did they have in general the imagination to deal with it in terms of outer space?

Adm. H.: The point I'm trying to make is that the Bureau had no charter, you might say, for that sort of experimentation, because the duties of the Bureau of Ordnance lay in other directions.

Q: Your son said a little while ago that when you returned to the Bureau of Ordnance in 1924 you discovered that various things had been dropped. The Goddard experiment was one, I take it. What else?

Adm. H.: That's the one that I had reference to. Did I say that various projects had been dropped?

Q: As I recall, your son intimated that there was more than one project that had been dropped. Perhaps I misunderstood.

Adm. H.: I would have to ask him what he had in mind because that's the only one that occurs to me, offhand.

Q: Were there other experiments in that period that engaged your interest?

Adm. H.: None, I think, that would be of any popular interest or consequence. We were always looking for ways to improve the performance of ordnance, whether it was guns, bombs, such items as fuses for live ammunition, torpedoes - although the torpedo section did most of its own direction of experiments.

The experimental section of the Bureau in those days had more to do perhaps with development of ammunitions more than anything else, when it comes right down to it.

Q: Did you work with the Bureau of Standards?

Adm. H.: Oh, yes, we had, as far as my end of it was concerned, a very happy relationship with the Bureau of Standards in those days. We consulted with them quite a bit, and they were very generous in their help. As a matter of fact, one of the people with whom we dealt in the Bureau of Standards became an employee of the Bureau of Ordnance and eventually went to the proving ground at Dahlgren as I suppose they called him a ballistician or a ballistics engineer, or something of that sort. The Bureau of Standards was always ready to help.

Q: What about your liaison with the Army, your counterparts over there?

Adm. H.: I don't think that my section of the Bureau of Ordnance had a real counterpart in the Army, but of course they had an explosives section in Army Ordnance and I think probably a counterpart to our aviation ordnance section. There was an interdepartmental ordnance board in those days with representatives from Army Ordnance and Navy Ordnance that met from time to time.

Q: Did you sit on that board?

Adm. H.: Yes. I was an ex officio member of that board when I was in charge of the experimental section. The Army was working along parallel lines with us in some respects. They had a great interest in the bombsight experimentation, although we were carrying on the Norden developments. Exchange of information and ideas with Army Ordnance was perfectly free and open.

Q: Did your position involve touring industry and visiting factories and that sort of thing?

Adm. H.: No, not very much because that would have to do primarily I think with the supply section of the Bureau, the sections that were responsible for overseeing the contracts for ordnance items. The experimental section had no supervision of contracts or that kind of thing. About the only contracts that I can recall the experimental section dealt with were personal-service contracts like the one with Dr. Goddard, the one with Carl Norden, and there were one or two others. There was a time when we had an experimental contract with DuPont Company for the production of so-called smokeless powder. That came under my division because it was an experimental project.

Does that answer your question?

Q: Yes, it does. Were you directly or indirectly, through Aeronautics, involved with lighter-than-air craft in any way?

Adm. H.: To the extent that lighter-than-air aircraft would need or would accommodate ordnance items, yes. As a matter of fact, that's a story of its own in my experience.

Q: Well, tell it to me.

Adm. H.: When the lighter-than-air dirigibles were under development during the early and mid 20s, it was presumed that they would eventually carry armament of some kind, even if only for self-protection, and that they would have use for pyrotechnic devices, for instance, for navigation, perhaps for signaling. So that, to my mind, the experimental section of the Bureau had an interest in the characteristics and operations of lighter-than-air craft.

So when in the summer of 1925 a cruise of the Shenandoah was projected, which was to be a cruise into the Middle West and back, it appeared to me that that might be a good opportunity for me to become acquainted with lighter-than-air so that, as head of the section for experiments - experimental ammunition, at least - in the Bureau of Ordnance, I would have a better conception of what the structure and characteristics and operations of lighter-than-air craft actually were. I proposed to the Chief of the Bureau of Ordnance that I be designated to go on that particular cruise of the Shenandoah as an observer for the Bureau of Ordnance. The Chief of Bureau fell in with the idea and the upshot was that I received orders from the Bureau of Personnel - then the Bureau of Navigation, I believe - to go to the Shenandoah, or go with the Shenandoah, as a passenger on that cruise.

My preparations were simple. All I had to do was get myself and some toilet gear aboard the Shenandoah before she left Lakehurst. I was all prepared to catch a train out of Washington the afternoon before the sailing date, and I had arranged with my wife to pick me up at the Navy Department with the family car and take me to the station to get a train that would give me a Lakehurst connection. Shortly before she was to arrive for the purpose of picking me up, I received a telephone call from Commander Lansdowne from Lakehurst saying, in effect, that he would appreciate it if I were able to have my orders altered, cancelling them so far as the impending cruise of the Shenandoah was concerned, and planning instead to be an observer on one of the trips later in that season.

I acceded immediately to his request and went to see the Chief of the Bureau of Ordnance to tell him of the circumstance and to ask his permission to go immediately to the Bureau of Personnel and arrange for cancellation of my orders. Admiral Block was Chief of the Bureau at that time and he gave me permission to do what I had requested, which I proceeded to do and managed to get my orders cancelled as of that day.

Well, the next morning I had not been in my office very many minutes when the door opened and Admiral Block walked in and he said, in effect, "I permitted you to get your orders cancelled yesterday, although I didn't much want to do it. You are lucky."

I said, "How's that, Admiral?" and he said:

"The Shenandoah crashed out in Ohio early this morning."

So that was the end of that story.

Q: Did you ever learn why Commander Lansdowne asked that you postpone your trip?

Adm. H.: Oh, yes. I should have brought that in. He told me that the reason for it was because practically all of the student officers attached to the station at Lakehurst for lighter-than-air training were wild to go on that cruise. He said "if your orders are cancelled and postponed I can take one of them."

My reply to him was yes, of course, Zack, I'll get my orders changed right away - get the orders cancelled right away. If it hadn't been for that circumstance I would have been a passenger in the Shenandoah that night.

Q: Did you go on the Akron or any other - ?

Adm. H.: No. As a matter of fact, I think that after the crash of the Shenandoah there were no further lighter-than-air flights for quite a considerable period, and I think that by the time the next one was definitely scheduled I had left the Bureau. That's my present recollection. There was no question of an upcoming flight during the remainder of my tour in the Bureau. I think neither the Macon nor Akron was actually making flights up to the time I left the Bureau, at least not that kind of flight..

Q: You say that there is one other item that you do recall?

Adm. H.: I think I have the years correct, in referring to the flight of the NC boats across the Atlantic, which I believe took place in the spring of 1927, while I was still in the Bureau, I had been working - or my section had been working on the production of certain pyrotechnic aids for the NC boats in navigating out of sight of landmarks. This was in specific preparation for the transatlantic flight of the NC boats, but that had nothing to do with my second tour in the Bureau.

Q: No, in May 1919, that being the first tour. But why don't you put it in at this point.

Hustvedt #3 - 105

Adm. H.: As long as the matter of the conflict of dates is taken care of.

Q: Yes.

Adm. H.: During the preparation of the NC boats for their transatlantic flight the Bureau of Ordnance, and specifically the experimental section, was called upon to provide them with a crude bit of pyrotechnics as an aid to navigation. At the time, it was called a float light and it worked like this: the float light would be properly set to ignite and dropped from the plane, after landing on the water it would float and give off a bright pyrotechnic light of enough duration so that the plane could make a run on it of sufficient duration to establish how much of a wind drift was affecting the plane at that particular point in its flight.

That was a totally new development and the experimental section of the Bureau was responsible for producing it. I remember that on one of the tests of functioning of the float light, we made a test run on the Potomac at night and A. C. Read, who commanded the NC-4 in the upcoming flight, went with me down to the river that evening to witness the test. We went to Dahlgren quite frequently for tests of experimental ordnance devices of one kind or another. Dahlgren was one of my regular destinations for making what you might call a field trip for tests. I was at Dahlgren frequently, and about as often as not I was flown down there by plane from the air station at Anacostia. On one or two of those occasions, when I was in a plane with dual controls, the pilot would give me the signal, hold up his hands, and I would fly as best I could from somewhere around Mount Vernon to rounding the last point before arriving at Dahlgren.

Q: That was the extent of your career as a naval aviator, was it?

Adm. H.: Just about the extent of it. I remember that one time after we had landed at Dahlgren - we always went down in a seaplane and we'd land on the river and the proving ground would send a boat to take us off - this one time when I had been at the controls a good part of the way the proving ground officer who met us when we came ashore in the boat, one of the first things he said was, "Who was at the controls when you came around Mathias Point?" I said very proudly, "I was." He said, "I thought so"!

I didn't come anywhere near qualifying as a flier nor did I have any intention of doing so. I remember that my wife appeared to be able to tell every time when I had been on a flight to Dahlgren and back when I came home from the office. She would say, "You've been flying, haven't you?" Of course, the point was she always detected my complexion. I'd have a little bit of wind burn because the planes that we made those flights in in those days were open-cockpit planes and you got plenty of wind.

Q: Did you have any connection with the Naval Gun Factory, down at the Navy Yard?

Adm. H.: Yes. The Experimental Ammunition Unit at the Naval Gun Factory was established during the time that I was chief of the experimental section in the Bureau, so I actually had something to do with the establishment of that unit and afterwards a great deal of communication with it because they were handling various experimental matters that came directly under my cognizance at the Bureau end.

Q: It was more or less your test center, was it not?

Adm. H.: Yes, it was. The Experimental Ammunition Unit at the Navy Yard and the proving ground at Dahlgren and, to a lesser extent, the powder factory at Indian Head - well, that's about all of the activities coming directly under the Bureau of Ordnance that I had contact with on almost a daily basis.

Q: Admiral, in May of 1927 you were detached from the Bureau of Ordnance and you went as gunnery officer on the USS Colorado.

Adm. H.: That's right. The Colorado at that time was in the Navy Yard in New York for a short period of overhaul and then proceeded to join the rest of the battleship division on the West Coast, based on Long Beach.

I was in the Colorado a year as gunnery officer and there were no events out of the ordinary, I think connected with that tour of duty.

Q: Was she a happy ship?

Adm. H.: I would say so, yes. As far as I was concerned, she was. The matter of happy ship or not largely depends upon the executive officer, I think, and we were lucky to have Frank J. Fletcher as our executive officer.

Q: Did you in that year take part in any war games or anything of the sort?

Adm. H.: Yes. In those days we had annually a fleet problem, which was a considerable war game. I don't remember much in detail about the fleet problem during the year I was in the Colorado. As a matter of fact, fleet problems, although they're interesting at the time, for some reason don't connect themselves in my mind with particular ships. I suppose that the reason for that is that the fleet problem involves the fleet. It doesn't involve an individual unit, It's an experience but somehow it doesn't attach itself to my mind to a particular ship that I may have been on at the time.

Q: Did you win a gunnery "E"?

Adm. H.: No, there were no gunnery "Es" connected with the Colorado at that time. At least, I don't recall any.

I went from gunnery officer of the Colorado to the staff of the Commander, Battleships, Pacific Fleet, as the Divisions' gunnery officer, on his staff. That was Admiral Nulton. There again I don't attach any special personal reminiscence to that tour of duty.

Admiral Nulton proceeded from command of battleships to Commander, Battle Fleet, and his staff by and large went with him, including myself.

Q: What was he like? I don't know very much about him.

Adm. H.: Admiral Nulton, as you know, was at one time Superintendent of the Naval Academy. He came to Commander, Battleship Division, in the West Virginia directly from being Superintendent of the Naval Academy.

Interview No. 4 with Vice Admiral Olaf M. Hustvedt, U.S. Navy
(Retired)

Place: His residence in Washington, D.C.

Date: Tuesday afternoon, 22 January 1974

Subject: Biography

By: John T. Mason, Jr.

Q: It's good to see you on this pre-spring day, Sir.

Adm. H.: Thank you.

Q: I think we're going to begin with the year 1927 when you were departing for the second time from the Bureau of Ordnance to go to sea.

Adm. H.: Yes, and that began my cruise at sea during which I was successively gunnery officer of the USS Colorado, staff gunnery officer on the staff of Commander, Battleship Divisions of the Battle Fleet, and moving with him, Admiral L. M. Nulton, when he became Commander-in-Chief of the Fleet, up to his Fleet flagship.

Q: Tell me first about the Colorado.

Adm. H.: There isn't very much to tell about the Colorado, except that she was participating actively in all of the fleet operations in the year I was in her. She had just finished an overhaul as I joined.

Q: Was she in the Pacific?

Adm. H.: No, in the Atlantic at that time, but moved to the Pacific. I joined the Colorado in the Navy Yard, New York. The Battle Fleet had been on the East Coast for fleet problems et cetera, and I joined just before the Colorado wound up a very short period of overhaul and proceeded singly to the West Coast to rejoin the Battle Fleet at the California bases.

I don't remember anything out of more or less routine with the Colorado other than taking part in fleet exercises, including the gunnery exercises et cetera.

Q: Did you win an "E"?

Adm. H.: No. I think that an individual gun or turret in the Colorado produced an "E" but the ship itself took no trophies.

Q: Did you carry a catapult and a plane?

Adm. H.: Yes. We had our complement of four light planes and a catapult on turret 3.

Q: Were the planes useful to you in gunnery practice?

Adm. H.: Oh, yes, surely, as spotting planes for the correction of gunfire.

Q: Did the Colorado have 16-inch guns?

Adm. H.: 14-inch guns - no, wait a minute, the Colorado had 16-inch guns, yes.

Q: The fleet exercises were carried on where? Off the California coast?

Adm. H.: The fleet exercises that year, as I remember it, were entirely in the Pacific. I don't remember that we got back into the Atlantic again during my year in the Colorado. In fact, I'm quite sure we didn't.

Q: That was the year 1927. Were you circumscribed in any way in the amount of ammunition you could use or anything of that sort?

Adm. H.: Well, of course, the gunnery exercises were carried out with the ammunition allowance prescribed for each gun or turret. There was no procurement in that direction. The ammunition allowance for the exercises was entirely normal, and the exercises themselves, I think, were all carried out during that year in accordance with the rules for gunnery exercises without any curtailment of the exercises themselves, either in number or character.

I think for the Battle Fleet that was, you might say, a very normal peacetime training year, the year of 1927-28. The years immediately following were, too.

Q: It was only when we got into the Great Depression that there was some curtailment?

Adm. H.: I don't recall that myself particularly because in the initial years of the Depression I was on shore duty at the Washington Navy Yard. I was not in the fleet. I don't recall any curtailment of the gunnery exercises on account of the Depression.

Q: You were only in the Colorado for a year and then you got promoted?

Adm. H.: I moved to the staff of the Commander, Battleship Divisions, who was at that time Vice Admiral L. M. Nulton, and after a year on his staff on the West Virginia I moved with him and the rest of the staff to California where he became Commander-in-Chief, Battle Fleet.

Q: Tell me what were your duties with him when he was Commander, Battleship Divisions. You were listed as his aide. What did that entail?

Adm. H.: As I recall it, the word "aide" was added to the orders of a certain limited number of the Admiral's staff.

The "aide," it's implied, is a personal sort - personal as well as official sort of assistant, whereas the staff of a flag officer afloat normally consists of quite a large group of officers and enlisted men, but there are very few of them that are designated as personal aides to the flag officer.

Q: They're just a little bit closer to the admiral?

Adm. H.: I suppose that's the general idea.

Q: As division gunnery officer what were your duties?

Adm. H.: They were largely concerned with the preparation of schedules for gunnery exercises, for the dissemination of information relating to gunnery, as it applied to our particular ships, and assistance generally in the laying out and issuance of operations orders. Of course, the staff gunnery officer didn't have primary responsibility or cognizance of operations, except in a contributory sense.

I don't think there was anything unusual about the staff service with the fleet at that time, other than going on pretty much in the same form for a good many years and I think did for a good many years afterwards.

Q: In this particular job, did it mean that you had to visit the various battleships in the division?

Adm. H.: Yes, in a general sense. Not with a schedule but

with quite frequent contact with the gunnery officers of the ships in the divisions and consultation with them regarding schedules, problems, and gunnery matters in general.

Q: Did you have the authority to point out to an individual gunnery officer some defect in his observation of regulations and that sort of thing?

Adm. H.: I had no command authority over individual gunnery officers. That's what you had in mind?

Q: Yes.

Adm. H.: Of course, we had discussions on various topics.

Q: When the division was at sea and you wanted to visit another battleship, how were you transported from one to the other? By high line?

Adm. H,: There wasn't very much of the high-line business going on in those days! Of course, those were peace years and the schedules were laid out pretty well in advance, and the movements were scheduled quite a bit in advance, as a rule. The operations were such that there wasn't much occasion for the transfer of any personnel from ship to ship at sea, and no fueling or provisioning at sea that I can recall during those years.

Q: It was a known technique, though, was it not?

Adm. H.: I don't think that back there in the 30s the technique was really advanced as it became advanced during the 40s, when groups of ships were at sea for weeks on end and were refueled and supplied at sea.

Q: Wartime made it expedient?

Adm. H.: Yes.

Q: But they were practicing with the technique a little bit?

Adm. H.: I don't recall just how that matter stood. Of course the techniques of communication were known for a long time and practiced occasionally, but in fleet operations of the late 30s I don't remember that we had occasion to use any of those techniques. Our schedules were pretty carefully mapped out and pretty closely adhered to, so that provisioning and fueling were taken care of in port and sufficed for the operations that were scheduled.

The business of fueling and provisioning at sea was more or less an emergency type of operation and of course it was very much practiced in wartime, but not normally in peacetime.

Q: When the fleet moved down to the Panama Canal Zone from California, what did destroyers do in the way of refueling, or did they have enough fuel on board to take them that distance?

Adm. H.: I think the destroyers had enough fuel on board to go from Californian ports, say, down to Panama, and from Panama to Guantanamo, from Guantanamo to the East Coast ports. I don't recall occasions when it was necessary to take a destroyer alongside a battleship for fueling in those days.

Q: Did you during this period when you were with Admiral Nulton have any exercises which involved the defense of the Panama Canal?

Adm. H.: Yes, we had at least one exercise, I think, during the time I was on Admiral Nulton's staff that involved the Panama area on the West Coast and also in the Caribbean area, including the Panama area itself.

The Fleet concentration, as it was called in those days, which brought together the principal operating units from both coasts and normally took place in the West Indies, sometimes involved waters not far from the Panama Canal. Of course, the fleet problems of that period were usually involving the Caribbean as a whole. If they were on the West Coast they sometimes involved Alaska and, of course, Hawaii.

Q: When you had a fleet problem that involved the Caribbean, did you take into consideration the possible assistance of our longtime ally, Britain, and the Royal Navy?

Adm. H.: Not in those days, as I recall it, because I think

to have done so would have involved designating some assembly or some organization of ships as representing the Blue or the Violet or the what not. I don't remember during those particular years that we had any fleet problems that involved that type of cooperation. I don't remember any from the late 20s and early 30s.

Q: Again, focusing on that Caribbean area and the fleet exercises, did the so-called Monroe Doctrine figure into the considerations of the Navy?

Adm. H.: I don't remember that it did, as such. Of course, the usual set-up involved two sides to the problem, but the sides were not so conceived, I think, or so stated or represented as to give a strong impression that this side represented Germany, let's say, or another side represented Britain, or anything of that kind. I don't recall any such problems - I mean problems that gave that tinge to the set-up.

Q: That came to be the case in the Pacific, did it not, where the Orange was usually thought of as Japanese?

Adm. H.: Oh, yes, I think problems that were set up in the Pacific involving, let's say, Alaskan waters and the Polynesian waters, I presume the natural thing was to view those problems in the light of being a possible situation as between ourselves and Japan. Very natural that it should in those days. There was no other considerable naval representation in the Pacific nor, I suppose, did we really conceive of any other possible confrontation in the Pacific.

Q: Thinking of the Panama Canal and exercises in defense of the canal, what role was assigned at that time to aircraft in protective measures?

Adm. H.: As far as the aircraft that I had anything to do with were concerned, the only aircraft that I had personally anything to do with were the scouting and spotting planes that we carried on the battleships. As gunnery officer in the Colorado, the planes came under my department, presumably because their principal function was assumed to be that of spotting for the correction of gunfire. Of course, the scouting function was recognized, naturally, and taken into account I think when fleet problems were set up.

Q: Tell me a little about Admiral Nulton. What was he like as a commander?

Adm. H.: Admiral Nulton came to us directly from being Superintendent of the Naval ACademy, and of course, he was a Virginia gentleman. His relations with his staff, as far as I can recall, were always pleasant and always on a high level.

Does that answer your question? I don't know just how

else I can —

Q: What I meant was was he an outstanding commander or was he a run-of-the-mill type?

Adm. H.: I should hesitate to attempt to render any judgment on that score. I know that he was liked and respected by his staff and, as far as I know, by the fleet in general. I would assume that his administration of the fleet was regarded as successful, seeing he was advanced from Commander, Battleships, in 1928-29, I think it was, to Commander-in-Chief, Battle Fleet, in 1929-30.

Q: That's rather stark evidence, is it not, of the fact?

Adm. H.: I would think so.

Q: Tell me, Sir, in that time or a little bit later, I know that there were problems with attempted espionage on the California coast, as it pertained to the fleet. Were there any in your time with the battleships?

Adm. H.: I don't remember ever learning of any, no. I don't remember even any suggestion or any whisper that anything of that sort was going on.

Q: It was a little bit later, when Admiral Joseph Mason Reeves was in command out there.

Adm. H.: Admiral Reeves was in command in —

Q: Immediately afterwards, wasn't he, in 1931 or thereabouts?

Adm. H.: I was going to say I think he must have come immediately after. Admiral de Steiguer was Commander, Battle Fleet, just before Admiral Nulton. My memory is a little off there, I think.

Q: During this period, 1929-30, was the Mississippi a unit of the Battleship Division? If so, was Tommy Hart there?

Adm. H.: I don't think the Mississippi was in the Battle Fleet at that time. The latest battleships in the Battle Fleet during the time that I was with Admiral Nulton were the California and Tennessee. The Colorado, Maryland, and West Virginia were later than they, but I mean prior to the Colorado, Maryland, and West Virginia type, I think the Tennessee and California were the latest to join the fleet - and the Arizona.

Q: What was the state of the base at San Diego in that time?

Adm. H.: During that period that we've just been dealing with, when I was in battleships, I literally didn't see San Diego. San Diego was the destroyer base and the base for the light cruisers and the base for aviation generally. When I was in the Battleship Divisions and was in gunnery in the Colorado, West Virginia, and California I don't remember being in San Diego at all, except going down there in a car.

Q: What was considered the base for the battleships?

Adm. H.: San Pedro-Long Beach. Oh, yes, decidedly.

Q: Did the fleet during this time go through Hawaii ever?

Adm. H.: I don't recall being in Hawaii during that particular period, which was 1927 to 1930. We're still talking about that period?

Q: Yes.

Adm. H.: No, I don't remember being in Hawaii then, on that particular cruise.

Q: But you did say that there was a fleet exercise which involved Alaska?

Adm. H.: I didn't mean to say that there was one involving Alaska during that particular period. No, I don't recall definitely that there was. As a matter of fact, the only fleet exercises that I remember involving a large area had to do with the Caribbean rather than anywhere in the Pacific. During these particular years, now, I'm talking about 1927 to 1930, and I'm talking about what I remember of them.

I remember a considerable fleet problem involving the Caribbean area during that period.

Q: What was the personnel situation with the fleet in that time?

Adm. H.: I would say that it was probably normal for a peacetime period. Of course, we're talking now about a period which was rather well after World War I and rather well before World War II.

Q: And economically we were -

Adm. H.: Strapped!

Q: We began to get into that period of being strapped, and I wondered if the fact that the country was going into a depression era if this was reflected in personnel problems in the fleet?

Adm. H.: I don't think it really was, as such.

Q: Well, Sir, you have told me about the fleet organization and things that pertain to units of the fleet. Now would you tell me about any personal experiences that you had in this time which do stand out?

Adm. H.: We are talking now about the period from 1927 to 1930, aren't we?

Q: Yes.

Adm. H.: No, I don't remember anything that really stood out.

Q: Was your family based in Long Beach?

Adm. H.: Yes, my family was living in Long Beach at that time. At the time, my wife's parents were living in Hemet, California, which was accessible, and my eldest brother who was a professor at the University of California, Los Angeles, was living in the Santa Monica area. So when it came to weekends we were quite often upcountry with Judge and Mrs. Cooper at their home just outside of Hemet and were also seeing a good deal of my brother and his family in the Santa Monica area.

Q: He was the philologist, was he?

Adm. H.: No, I wouldn't say that he was a philologist, as such. He was in the English Department at UCLA, and I think at this time, 1927 to 1930, he really occupied the position of being next to the head of the department.

That's about all I remember as a general personal comment on that particular period.

Q: It seems like a happy set of circumstances that your family was not buffeted from pillar to post. I mean your duties were in Washington and then with the fleet, but in such a way that you could be with your family a good deal of the time?

Adm. H.: Yes. Of course, that base at San Pedro-Long Beach for the battleships was really a secure home base, you might say. We were there with a good deal of regularity. Of course, if we went to the Caribbean for a period of three months that meant we were away. If we went to the Navy Yard for an overhaul that was likely to be another separation because the battleships in those days were based on the Navy Yard in Bremerton to be overhauled.

Q: Were many of the officers fortunate enough to be provided with quarters?

Adm. H.: Officers of the fleet? Officers of the fleet were never provided with quarters at that time.

Q: Quarters, as such, were very few and far between?

Adm. H.: There were quarters at naval stations, such as the Navy Yards, Mare Island, Bremerton. I think there was nothing much in the way of quarters in the San Diego area at that time. The Naval Air Station, I suppose, yes. Otherwise I don't recall any.

Q: Well, Sir, after that period with the fleet in the Pacific you came back to Washington once again?

Adm. H.: Yes, I came back to the Naval Gun Factory, which was in line with my having been given some education in naval ordnance. I was sent to shore duty at a naval ordnance establishment.

Q: It seems like a great consistency in your assignment.

Adm. H.: When I went to the Naval Gun Factory I was at first, for some six or eight months, as I recall it, the Assistant Production Officer, the Production Officer at that time being Commander David Ducey, who was a class ahead of mine. During the second year I was there, Commander Ducey was detached to other duty and I became the Production Officer at the Naval Gun Factory during the years from 1931 to 1933. I was there initially in the summer of 1930, and from 1931 to 1933 I was the Production Officer.

Q: What percentage of the guns required by the fleet were manufactured at the Naval Gun Factory?

Adm. H.: I'd be hard put to answer that as a percentage. A rather overwhelming majority of them were, I think.

Q: Was there another naval gun factory located elsewhere in the country?

Adm. H.: No. The Army had its Watervliet Arsenal and Bethlehem at Midvale was in the business of producing guns up to large calibers, but most of the guns for the fleet were actually produced at the Naval Gun Factory in those days.

Q: Including the very-large-caliber ones?

Adm. H.: Including the 16-inch.

Q: What about the men whom you employed in the Gun Factory?

Were they Civil Service?

Adm. H.: Yes, they were Civil Service people, including engineers and draftsmen who were certainly in the top reaches of Civil Service as far as compensation is concerned.

Q: Then, I take it you had no problems ever with labor?

Adm. H.: During the years that I was there, 1930 to 1933, production was pretty well on an even keel so that labor problems were practically at a minimum, I would say. There was not a serious disruption in the labor force at the Gun Factory during those years. Of course, the load in various shops varied to a certain extent so that there was a bit of shuffling of personnel between shops, depending upon their specialties and the work load of the time, but nothing very serious. Things were pretty much on an even keel, I think, at the Gun Factory in 1930 to 1933.

Q: Didn't you experience some drastic limitations of money?

Adm. H.: We had money to carry on the functions that were in our province at that time, which was supplying ordnance materials to the fleet and to new construction. I don't recall anything in the nature of an upheaval in our work load during those years.

Q: Were there any new type guns coming on stream?

Adm. H.: Well, the new types involved antiaircraft guns

rather than other types. There were big-gun ships coming on over the horizon, the ships that led off with the North Carolina, but the production for those ships was not affecting the work load at the Naval Gun Factory in the early 30s.

Q: What type of antiaircraft gun were we manufacturing and using in the early 30s?

Adm. H.: I think the 5-inch AA gun had not yet come into production so that the actual antiaircraft guns of the early 30s were more of the character of machine guns. I don't recall that we had any 5-inch antiaircraft guns in our program between 1930 and 1933.

Q: Were the several treaties on limitation of armament specific about guns on warships?

Adm. H.: Not that I recall.

Q: Did you live at the Navy Yard?

Adm. H.: Yes, that was the one place during my naval career that I occupied public quarters. During my days as a student officer in ordnance I was attached to the proving ground at Indian Head for a period of seven or eight months and during a part of that time I had lived in the bachelor officers' quarters. During the last five months or so I was given quarters through the courtesy of the supply officer who was a bachelor and who went to live with the proof officer, who was also a bachelor, and my family and I lived in the supply officer's quarters for about five months. That little period and my period of three years at the Naval Gun Factory were the only periods during my career when I occupied public quarters with my family.

Q: That's what I was getting at earlier when I brought up the subject of quarters, the rarity of such an experience in a man's career.

As head of the Naval Gun Factory, did you get involved with the proving grounds or anything of this sort?

Adm. H.: In the first place, I was not head of the Naval Gun Factory. I was the Production Officer.

Q: The operational man!

Adm. H.: In a sense, yes. As far as the Gun Factory is concerned, I was the third in command. There was the Commandant of the Navy Yard, who was also Superintendent of the Gun Factory, then there was the Senior Assistant to the Commandant, and then there was the Production Officer. So I was never in command of the Gun Factory except technically for a few hours now and then in the absence of my two seniors.

Q: How did you like being a production chief?

Adm. H.: I enjoyed that experience and I think it was a beneficial experience and it was a pleasant experience on the whole. There were no serious hitches that come to my mind now, so I think that on the whole things ran rather smoothly at the Gun Factory in those days.

Q: Did you have any particular difficulty in securing the necessary amount of steel?

Adm. H.: No, I don't recall any difficulty with that item.

Q: What complement of personnel would you have at the Naval Gun Factory?

Adm. H.: That's something on which I can't give you a categorical answer nor a particularly accurate guess. I would say, if it came to a guess, that the Naval Gun Factory at that time was employing somewhere in the neighborhood of 2,000 men, but I'm sorry to say that's a guess. I don't think it was anything less than that.

Q: What were your relations with the Army people next door?

Adm. H.: You mean the Army people who were also in the Washington Area?

Q: Yes, at Fort McNair.

Adm. H.: The Army War College and so on. We had very little

contact with them. I would say that at the Gun Factory we probably had no more contact with the Army there than with the Army at Fort Myer, because they had no manufacturing functions there so our activities didn't mesh.

Q: You moved in different orbits?

Adm. H.: Yes.

Q: That was a very exciting period in Washington with the Depression hitting hard, and one notable event that comes to mind was the Bonus Army. Tell me about your observations of that from the vantage point of the Navy Yard.

Adm. H.: Our connection with the Bonus Army events was very sketchy. Of course, what was going on in town in connection with the Bonus Army was not touching us down at the Washington Navy Yard, except as we read in the papers what was going on. But when the crunch came and the Bonus marchers were evicted from their camp sites uptown and were herded together, they were herded down past the Washington Navy Yard and across the Anacostia River, by way of the bridge adjacent to the Navy Yard, and put into a camp of sorts over on the Anacostia Flats. That brought the "Army" on the march right past the Navy Yard gates and, of course, the situation throughout that part of town was rather tense. Nobody knew just what to expect from the Bonus marchers under the conditions, but the movement was carried out without disturbing us inside the Navy Yard wall particularly. It was an event and a movement which was on our doorstep that didn't affect our routine.

Q: It was also an event that was potentially more dangerous than it turned out to be.

Adm. H.: Yes, that's true. It could have been a catastrophe.

Q: What relationship did you have, when you were at the Navy Yard and the Gun Factory, with your old office in BuOrd, the experimental section?

Adm. H.: Well, the Experimental Ammunition UNit was carrying out its business during the time I was in the Navy Yard, but it was doing most of its business in close liaison with the two desks in the Bureau that were particularly concerned with experimental work, that is, the experimental section of the Bureau and the mines section of the Bureau. The building in which it operated was initially planned as a mine building and at the time I was in the Yard it housed the experimental mine unit and the experimental ammunition unit. As I say, their liaison with the two desks concerned in the Bureau was pretty close and in that respect they were in some degree independent of the Naval Gun Factory administration.

Q: Were guns manufactured by the Gun Factory installed in the WAshington Navy Yard in warships, or were they shipped elsewhere?

Adm. H.: They were shipped elsewhere for mounting on board ship.

Q: Was that also your province?

Adm. H.: Not the shipping and distribution, no. My province had to do with the work that was performed in the shops, in assembling and rifling the guns.

Q: In every job there's something that's less than perfect. There must have been some headaches that you experienced in the manufacture of guns?

Adm. H.: The Washington Navy Yard Naval Gun Factory had been making guns for a great many years before I ever arrived on the scene and the technology was pretty well established before I ever got there, so far as the manufacture of guns was concerned, the assembly of gun tubes and liners and hoops and the various components of the guns and the cutting of the rifling grooves. Those were pretty-well-established technologies before I ever appeared on the scene. I don't recall any great technical problems arising during the time I was there.

Q: How did you master these technical problems as a producer of guns? Was there a breaking-in period, or had your previous experience in the Department taught you all that was necessary?

Adm. H.: Well, of course, when I went to the WAshington Navy Yard the technique of manufacturing guns, assembling the components of the gun itself, the liners, and the hoops, and the cutting of the rifling grooves, and that sort of thing, was a technique that had been under development for years and had reached a high state of the art so far as the Naval Gun Factory was concerned. There was little, you might say, that remained experimental in the manufacture of rifled guns.

Q: But as a new Production Manager how did you master all of this?

Adm. H.: My function was really so far as the manufacture of guns was concerned was to see that the existing organization continued to roll the way it had been rolling! There was very little that was required on my part.

Q: Except did it not require a comprehensive knowledge on your part?

Adm. H.: It required a knowledge of the processes and the elements concerned and the kind of material concerned and the type of workmanship concerned, that sort of thing, but it didn't require any innovations on my part so far as the assembling of a gun was concerned. The technique had been highly developed before I ever got there.

Q: But how did you acquire this knowledge of the highly

developed technique? Not by osmosis!

Adm. H.: No. Assuming that I had acquired it, the function that I was performing was, you might say, one of keeping in touch with the shop operations to ensure that they were being supervised by the skilled technicians who were in charge of them and to supply an upper management function that was somewhat removed from the intimate technical details of overseeing the work of individual machines or operators, because the organization itself contained the necessary personnel to keep the machinery running and to ensure that the operations were in accordance with the drawings et cetera.

My function was more related to personnel management than it was to the technical aspects of machining gun parts and assembling them. I was not required to be a gun designer. I was not required to be a draftsman of any kind. I was an overseer, if you please, who spent a good part of his time in an office taking care of the office business which is connected with any manufacturing establishment, any establishment producing a technical product.

Q: I take it, then, Sir, that in the realm of personnel is where we see the skill of an officer who is trained to command converge more or less with the management function of a gun factory, it's in the realm of personnel?

Adm. H.: Of course, the shops at the Gun Factory were each headed by a shop superintendent who was a man of long experience in the particular functions being performed by the shop which he headed as a foreman. So when a purely technical question would arise in the shop, the superintendent of the shop had access to other experts in the organization who were designers, engineers, draftsmen, with whom they could consult in regard to details. The management set-up of the Gun Factory included inspectors who were in touch with the work that was going on in the various shops connected with producing the particular specialty for which they were qualified as inspectors, inspectors of the workmanship, inspectors of the compliance with drawings, inspectors of attaining the proper finishes, that sort of thing.

The production officer had an office which comprised a force of draftsmen, inspectors, who were his representatives throughout the plant in dealing with problems that were arising in the plant in regard to compliance with the drawings and specifications et cetera. The function of the production officer was to be a sort of topside manager of that organization. Of course, there might be problems that would arise as between a shop superintendent and the inspector which in the end might have to be brought to the production officer and laid before him with the question of what to do, what's the answer. Those things, fortunately, arose rarely because the whole organization was an organization of experts with long experience and high capabilities, and the way in which the production proceeded and the way it was coordinated, inspected, and so on was an organization of long standing and of experience and expertness, and the problems that arose were usually capable of being solved without any great amount of controversy.

You get what I mean?

Q: Yes, I do.

Adm. H.: That was a going concern with long-established processes, mostly, and long-established relationships between the shop force and the inspection force and so on. The actual problems arising were usually technical not problems of principle, you might say, and technical problems whose solutions lay along pretty-well-known lines.

Do I make myself clear?

Q: Yes. Was there any cooperation between private industry and the Naval Gun Factory, between the Naval Gun Factory and outfits like that at Springfield, the Springfield Rifle people? Was there any cooperation or any liaison?

Adm. H.: If I get you correctly, there was the cooperation that would exist between organizations which were performing the same sort of function but not really in competition with each other. More a cooperative type of relationship, rather than competitive.

Q: Yes, well, one was government and the other was private.

Adm. H.: Yes, and when it came to the manufacture of ordnance the way in which the business, so to speak, was divided up had been a matter of pretty long standing, and the people concerned knew each other pretty well and realized - I suppose had come to realize through their experience - that the only possible path for them was cooperation, and the cooperation was there. There wasn't any throat-cutting between the Naval Gun Factory and Bethlehem Steel, for instance, or Midvale, that sort of thing.

Q: How many different kinds of guns approximately would the Naval Gun Factory turn out?

Adm. H.: That would be hard to answer. Probably six, eight, or ten different calibers, not necessarily all at the same time.

Q: Is the title "Naval Gun Factory" a true title, or were other items of ordnance manufactured there?

Adm. H.: Oh, yes, the Naval Gun Factory at the Washington Naval Yard made optical instruments, for one thing. It had an optical shop that was a part of the Gun Factory. Optics were really the principal thing other than guns. Guns and gun mounts, of course, but primarily guns.

Q: In a sense the Navy, in operating this factory, was in competition with private industry, was it not?

Adm. H.: It was in the sense that the Bethlehem Steel Company also made naval guns. Midvale was concerned with armor really more than with guns. I think it was a good thing that the government had competition from private manufacturers of ordnance. Of course, the Army was making its own guns, too, to a degree at Watervliet Arsenal.

Interview No. 5 with Vice Admiral Olaf M. Hustvedt, U.S. Navy
(Retired)

Place: His residence in Washington, D.C.

Date: Tuesday afternoon, 12 February 1974

Subject: Biography

By: John T. Mason, Jr.

Q: Well, Sir, even though I came by surprise today, I look forward to another interesting chapter. Last time, you broke off as you concluded your tour of duty at the Naval Gun Factory, and I think you had been assigned as executive officer to the USS Louisville. Will you pick up the story at that point, Sir?

Adm. H.: That was, I believe, in 1933. Do you have the date?

Q: That's right, it was, and you served in her from 1933 to 1935.

Adm. H.: Yes. That was one of the occasions when I was able to change duty and place of abode for my family and accompany the family during the shift. That didn't always happen.

Q: Where was the Louisville? On the Pacific coast?

Adm. H.: The <u>Louisville</u> at that time when I joined her happened to be in San Francisco Bay, but she was normally based on the San Pedro-Long Beach port.

Q: Did you travel by automobile across the country?

Adm. H.: We traveled by automobile, the whole family, from Washington to Long Beach, and it so happened we were able to move into a house in Long Beach which we had occupied during my previous tour of sea duty based on San Pedro-Long Beach, so the move was about as painless as any family move can be.

Q: You must have liked that house?

Adm. H.: Oh, yes, we did. We found it a convenient and commodious sort of house for our family.

Q: Did you have any trials and tribulations on the cross-country trip?

Adm. H.: No, I don't remember any on that particular trip. I think that was one of the smooth ones, really.

Q: What were the roads like in that time?

Adm. H.: The roads were generally quite passable, if one stuck to the main roads and didn't have too many diversions en route. I don't recall any difficulties at all during that particular trip. I landed the family at Long Beach at the house that we were familiar with and caught one of the passenger ships to San Francisco. The Yale and Harvard were operating along the coast at that time, and I went up in one of them. I've forgotten which one.

Q: What line was that?

Adm. H.: I don't even remember the name of the line. I think it was an independent line, so far as the name was concerned. I don't know whether it was a Matson subsidiary or a Union Pacific subsidiary, or what it was. It was ostensibly, I think, an independent line, and the only ships that it was operating as far as I'm aware were that pair, the Yale and Harvard, on the San Francisco-Los Angeles run. The service was quite frequent and quite a good service.

I recall arriving at San Francisco and reporting aboard the Louisville on Memorial Day, not that that made any special difference. My cruise on the Louisville was on the whole a very agreeable one largely, I think, because of the commanding officers we had there. The first one being Captain Bruce Kanega and his relief during approximately my second year on board being George V. Stewart. During part of that period the Louisville was a flagship of cruisers - of a cruiser division. The period I can't recall very accurately, but Admiral Thomas C. Hart was the second of those flag officers, and it was during his incumbency, as I recall it, that we participated in a fleet problem which took the Louisville to an initial position at Dutch Harbor, in the Aleutians. That, of course, was an interesting departure, since most of our previous problems had had to do with the tropics, rather than with Alaska.

Q: I take it this was a problem that was worked out in the summertime?

Adm. H.: No, I think that problem ran approximately from March to May.

Q: And the problem was the fleet defense of Alaska, was it?

Adm. H.: A fleet problem in which the force that the Louisville was attached to started the problem from a position in the Aleutians. I'm not too clear about the details of that particular problem. I remember the dates only rather sketchily as the spring of 1935, but perhaps that's jumping ahead a little too fast for your purposes. Is it?

Q: Yes. Tell me, the Louisville was a heavy cruiser, was she?

Adm. H.: A heavy cruiser, yes. Her main armament 8-inch guns in turrets.

Q: When Bruce Kanega was captain did you see anything of Nimitz?

Adm. H.: I don't recall that we did. Of course, Bruce Kanega and Nimitz were classmates and very close friends. But I remember another classmate of Captain Canaga who was also a commanding officer in the heavy cruiser squadron, H. Fairfax Leary, commanding the Indianapolis.

Q: Prior to the exercise in Alaskan waters, had you engaged in any other exercise?

Adm. H.: That particular fleet exercise came during my second year in the Louisville and it's my recollection that during the first year — yes, I'm sure it was during the first year — the fleet problem in which we took part was carried out in the Caribbean. That's going back a year.

One of the interesting things connected with our stay in the Caribbean in 1934 was that the Assistant Secretary of the Navy, who was Colonel Roosevelt, a former Marine officer, came down to make an inspection of sorts, I suppose, and was quartered on board the Louisville during the problem and at the conclusion of the problem the Louisville made a very quick little circuit in the West Indies to take Colonel Roosevelt to some of the places where he had served during his active Marine Corps career. We took him, as I remember it, first to San Juan, Puerto Rico, and from there to Cap Haitian in Haiti. He had served, I believe, with the Marines in Haiti during his days in the Marine Corps, and we went from Cap Haitian around to Port au Prince, and from Port au

Prince we joined the rest of the fleet, which had moved up to the U.S. east coast. We joined up in New York, in the Hudson River.

I remember that we also visited Narragansett Bay and Bar Harbor during that summer, and on our way back to the West Coast the _Louisville_ was detailed to visit Mobile, Alabama, in connection with an observance of some occasion at Mobile. I don't remember exactly what the occasion was. We were in Mobile for several days.

Q: Sometimes called the Flower Circuit, was it?

Adm. H.: Yes, something of that kind, I'm sure!.

Q: Colonel Roosevelt, was this TR Jr., or was it Kermit?

Adm. H.: Oh, no. He's a cousin of those Roosevelts and also a cousin of FDR. I can't tell you very much about his immediate family or his exact relationship to the two presidents of that name, but he did belong to the same family.

Q: Well, that was an extended exercise and tour, wasn't it, taking up most of the summer? And you left your family in Long Beach?

Adm. H.: No, my family came east that summer, and it was during that summer that we bought this present house, where we are at this moment. The family stayed here during the year after that. I think that was largely on account of the fact that the public schools in Long Beach were somewhat disrupted as a result of the earthquake which took place I believe quite early in 1933. When we moved out there in the summer of 1933, the results of the earthquake were still very evident although it hadn't affected the house that we were accustomed to living in in Long Beach, but it affected the public schools quite severely. I suppose that on account of the character of construction of the schools, with large classrooms, large hallways, and that sort of thing and the moderate climate for which they were built, they were not specially rugged, certainly not earthquake-proof because they were by and large rather severely damaged. Our children had to attend classes largely in temporary quarters.

Q: It turned out to be a very wise move, did it not, to buy a house in Washington?

Adm. H.: Oh, yes, indeed it did. It's been a very satisfactory arrangement because I still had a couple of tours of duty in Washington which involved finding a place to live and in the end it proved to be a very suitable and satisfactory place for retirement.

Q: At the moment it must have been something of a wrench for you, however, to have your family in Washington and you were still stationed out on the West Coast?

Adm. H.: Yes, that was, but it was something that wasn't too rare during other tours of sea duty. I was still on sea duty, you see, and whereas we returned to the Pacific from the East Coast in the early fall I was detached, as I remember it, in May, the following May, so that the actual separation was probably on the order of some eight months.

Q: Did you, along with all the others, suffer the 15 percent cut in pay?

Adm. H.: Oh, yes, but that had come, as I remember it, at the time I was still attached to the Gun Factory. I left the Gun Factory in May of 1933 and I think that cut had been in effect for some time in 1933.

Q: Tell me about Admiral Tommy Hart? How was he as a division commander?

Adm. H.: I would say that he was always very alert and very much abreast of what was going on around him. Sofar as his being in the ship with his staff is concerned, as far as I recall and as far as I was aware, relations of Admiral Hart and his staff with the ship and her captain and other personnel were agreeable ones. I remember Admiral Hart taking a close interest in the ship and what was going on, as well as keeping an eye on the rest of his command. The relationship was very agreeable sofar as I was concerned.

Q: When you went on this exercise to the Alaskan waters, in retrospect, you were dealing with a potential enemy, I take it, was there any similarity between your exercise then and what actually happened when the Japanese invaded the Aleutians?

Adm. H.: No, I can't say that I can recall any striking similarities. I don't remember too much of the details of that particular problem. We in our force up there in Alaska finally wound up somewhere near Hawaii, but as to the details of the problem I don't recall them distinctly.

Q: In that time was there ever any thought of a possible attack by an enemy through the Bering Sea?

Adm. H.: I can't answer that question categorically. I presume that there must have been in the strategic considerations that were kept in mind. As I say, I don't remember very much about the details of that particular problem. I do recall that apparently there were people in this country who took exception to our holding a fleet problem in that particular area at that particular time, because when I was detached from the Louisville, a very few months later, and reported in Washington I was assigned to the central division in the office of the Chief of Naval Operations and I remember that during the first few weeks I was there, or possibly the first few months, the central division was given a perfect flood of correspondence to acknowledge coming from people in various parts of the country protesting the Navy's holding a fleet problem in that part of the world at that particular time. I got the impression that there were speakers at various citizen meetings throughout the country who were urging their audiences to write letters of protest to the President and the Secretary of the Navy and so on protesting our holding that exercise in the area we did at the time we did, because they evidently thought that it would be a matter of provocation to Japan. As it so happened the character of some of those letters made it perfectly evident that the writers had attended meetings of some kind at which they had been urged to write letters of protest.

The way the protests were expressed was such that the source of their inspiration was perfectly apparent. Some of them were even subject to such errors of language that it was quite apparent that the people who wrote them didn't have very much idea of what they were doing but were following and getting their inspiration from someone else.

I remember one letter, for instance, which said that the writer protested the holding of naval maneuvers - I think it actually read "sending our fleet to the Allusion Idleness." Now nobody would write that letter unless a speaker on a platform had mentioned the Aleutian Islands. Do you think so?

Q: No. Consequently, how much credence did you place in these letters?

Adm. H.: Well, of course, the job that I had was to see that they were acknowledged and, at the time I arrived there in the Department, the actual maneuvers were behind us a matter of a couple of months, so this was a delayed reaction.

As I say, I couldn't escape the conclusion that practically all of those letters were written at the urging of somebody who had made a speech, given a talk, somewhere, and that well-meaning people were responding to a public urge to protest.

Q: Was any attempt made to discover who these people were who tried to stir up the protest? I mean, were they isolationists?

Adm. H.: That I can't answer.

Q: Were they isolationists?

Adm. H.: Presumably. The speakers concerned were, I imagine, isolationists of a perhaps rather fanatical kind. They'd been addressing public gatherings somewhere.

Q: Chautauqua Circuit, probably!

Adm. H.: Yes.

Q: This reflected a very strong attitude in the country in the middle thirties, did it not?

Adm. H.: I presume it did, yes. Otherwise, I don't know why there should have been public meetings in which the topic was brought up. But I had not been aware of the fact that there was any particular public attitude of protest, because I don't think that I had noticed it in the press. Of course, there may have been a flurry of protest about the thing at just the time when the maneuvers were under way and when we in the fleet didn't see the public press.

Q: I wonder if there was any protest in the Congress itself?

Adm. H.: That I couldn't tell you.

Q: That would have been more immediate, when you were still out.

Adm. H.: I really don't know, but evidently there were speakers addressing public meetings in protest.

Q: Does this sort of protest, collectively speaking, influence the Navy in its operational plans?

Adm. H.: Not to my knowledge. I don't think that that particular protest that I'm speaking of could have been extremely widespread and I don't remember gathering any impression that would lead me to put a finger on the source of those protests.

Q: That's very interesting.

You came back, you say, to become director of the Central Division. Tell me about the Central Division in the Navy Department.

Adm. H.: The Central Division was an adjunct of the office of the Chief of Naval Operations and it was what you might call the right-hand catchall division. It was located physically right next to the office of the Chief of Naval Operations himself. The only thing that separated the head of the Central Division from the Chief of Naval Operations was the office of the aides to CNO. The Central Division had the duty of maintaining, you might say, liaison with other government departments. It had supervision of the file rooms, the correspondence, of the Chief of Naval Operations.

We were the funnel, so to speak, for communications from other departments. One of the duties that fell to the chief of the Central Division was to attend a weekly conference in the State Department, which was set up to provide a regular and routine point of contact between the State Department and the military departments, War and Navy. A regular weekly meeting took place at the State Department with their representative, representatives from the War Department, and a representative from the Navy Department, who was, at that time, the chief of the Central Division.

Q: Did you share intelligence from the three branches of government?

Adm. H.: Well, that particular meeting was set up as a means of maintaining a quite frequent and routine contact between the State Department and the two military departments.

Q: It was active liaison, then?

Hustvedt #5 -153

Adm. H.: Yes-

Q: Then were you obligated to report to the Secretary of the Navy on anything that you gleaned from these meetings?

Adm. H.: In case it seemed necessary. Of course, our primary senior was the Chief of Naval Operations. It was our function to keep the Chief of Naval Operations advised of anything that came up in those meetings that seemed to be suitable for him to be cognizant of at the time.

Q: Can you give me an illustration of the type of information you received at these meetings?

Adm. H.: I remember one thing that was quite active at the time I was head of the office. I don't think I made it clear that when I first went to that office I didn't go there as the head. The head of the office at that time was Captain Bruce Canaga and I was the next senior, but when Captain Canaga was detached, after approximately a year, I became head of the division, and it was during the time that I was head of the division that I attended these joint sessions at the State Department.

One thing that was going on at that time was the disturbance in China.

Q: And that was in 1937?

Adm. H.: 1937, I think, is correct. That was at the time when there was a considerable degree of turmoil in China, and I think

Japan was stirring, too, at that time, wasn't it?

Q: Yes.

Adm. H.: It was the period when there was an attack on some of our ships in the Yangtze.

Q: The Panay?

Adm. H.: Yes, it was during that period.

Q: The State Department must have been very much exercised over that?

Adm. H.: Oh, yes, and that is possibly the reason that that regular weekly liaison was set up at that time, although I can't state that definitely. It may have been going on in the period before that, too.

Q: Did your Central Division have anything to do with the Congress? Did you receive letters in protest from the Congress on this and that?

Adm. H.: No, I don't remember anything relating to a direct liaison with Congress. Of course, the Navy Department had a liaison office set up with Congress, with an office up at the Capitol. The Central Division had nothing to do with that particular thing.

Q: I wondered. There's always a flood of congressional mail, and I wondered if that had come in to the Central Division?

Hustvedt #5 - 155

Adm. H.: The flood of mail that I was talking about?

Q: No.

Adm. H.: I don't recall that the Central Division was responsible for any of the liaison with Congress because the Navy Department had a liaison office actually at the Capitol in those days, with an officer of fair seniority in charge of it.

Q: Did you have anything to do with departmental publicity? Was that under your wing?

Adm. H.: No, but among the liaison functions was a liaison with the White House in matters of a rather routine character.

Q: What sort of things?

Adm. H.: Well, I recall that one of the things that happened during my time in the Central Division was the rather serious flooding in the Ohio Valley and the Navy Department was directed by the White House to send all available assistance to the flooded areas along the Ohio, even to sending boats out there. That was one of the things that came up that involved a direct White House liaison in matters of details. I recall that at that time I was on the telephone fairly frequently not only with the naval aide in the White House but with the White House press office, which was also a point of contact in regard to the movement of Navy assistance out to the flooded area. That was the only occasion that I can remember when contact of the Central Division with the White House was really active, not only daily but a number of times a day for a brief period.

Of course, there were very few matters in which the Central Division would properly have any liaison with the White House. This was a matter of handling an emergency.

Q: In that day, the Chief of Naval Operations was in direct command of the fleet. Did any of that brush off into any of the work involved in that brush-off to the Central Division?

Adm. H.: No, not really, because there were other offices in the organization. There was an office of Ships' Movements, for instance, and an office that handled the matter of material readiness, and so on. The Central Division was sort of a catch-all grab bag in a way. It handled the matters that didn't have any established home anywhere else.

Q: How large a staff did you have there?

Adm. H.: When I first went there the office consisted of the Director and about four assistant officers and, I believe, two clerk stenographers. That was about it. I think it stayed just about that way during the two years I was there. Of course, when war came on it may have been very much enlarged, but I was gone by that time.

Q: Did you have any kind of a liaison or relationship with the General Board? I know the General Board was under the control of the Secretary of the Navy but, nevertheless, related to the CNO.

Adm. H.: No, the Central Division had no function with relation to the General Board.

Q: Nevertheless, that must have been an interesting tour of duty. Your finger was on the pulse of the Navy in many ways, was it not?

Adm. H.: Yes, it was and, on account of the fact that it was a grab bag, it involved to some extent contacts that were out of the regular line. It was interesting and varied duties, as far as that's concerned.

Q: Was Admiral Leahy the Chief of Naval Operations?

Adm. H.: I think Admiral Leahy was the Chief practically all the time that I was in the Central Division.

Q: What was he like to work for?

Adm. H.: Oh, he couldn't have been better. It's my recollection that Admiral Standley was there part of the time, but I would have to refresh my memory on that. I think he was.

Q: Yes, he preceded Leahy. He was quite a different person, wasn't he?

Adm. H.: Well, yes. The contact of the Central Division with the Chief of Naval Operations himself was not exceedingly close because the aides' office was in between.

Q: Kind of a buffer!

Adm. H.: Not only officially but physically. The office of the adies was next to the office of the Chief and the Central Division was a couple of rooms beyond, so that the physical contact with the Chief of Naval Operations ran through the aides' office.

Q: Tell me what life was like in the old Navy Department in that time. You didn't have air-conditioning.

Adm. H.: I don't think we missed it particularly!

Q: It was something you'd never had, so you didn't miss it!

Adm. H.: That's right.

Q: But it must have been mighty uncomfortable there in that old building in the summertime?

Adm. H.: I don't remember suffering, really. We must have had desk fans and that sort of thing. We got along without too much discomfort, I believe.

The Chief of Naval Operations being on the front corridor, on the north side, and on the second floor, was probably in the most comfortable part of the building physically.

Q: He undoubtedly was!

Adm. H.: I don't remember having any particular great discomfort there. I presume we had our fans and we had the awnings, and so on and so forth.

Q: Did you have any outstanding crisis during your time in that office? Can you think of anything of that sort?

Adm. H.: No, but of course that attack on the Panay made a flurry, but I don't remember that it was anything earth-shaking. I presume that was the closest thing we had to an actual crisis during that period when I was in the office.

Q: What was the state of concern on the part of the Navy in that period towards a possible conflict with Japan?

Adm. H.: I don't remember that there was any crisis atmosphere during the time that I was there. As I said, the Panay incident was the closest. Naturally, we had realized for a considerable time that the Pacific was our critical area, but I don't recall any atmosphere of tension during the time that I was in that office.

Q: A study had been made around that time of the various islands in the Pacific and I believe the recommendation was made that we should go ahead and fortify some of these islands like Guam. Did that have its repercussions as far as your office was concerned?

Adm. H.: Not in the Central Divison that I can recall. We're talking about –

Q: The mid-thirties.

Adm. H.: No, I think the Panay incident came the closest to creating tension. I left there in 1937, as I recall.

Q: 1938.

Adm. H.: That's right, in 1938.

Q: You left to take command of the Detroit. Was she a heavy cruiser?

Adm. H.: No, she was a light cruiser, one of the so-called 10,000-tonners.

Q: So-called?

Adm. H.: Well, that was her approximate displacement.

Q: I wondered if there was a convertibility to a much more formidable warship?

Adm. H.: No, I don't think there was any practicability or any intention to make that class of cruisers convertible.

Q: Tell me where she operated. Tell me something about that tour of duty.

Adm. H.: The Detroit at that time was the flagship of Destroyers, Pacific Fleet, and she was the flagship of Admiral W. J. Sexton, who was Commander, Destroyers. I was in her for a year, in which we operated mostly out of San

Diego Harbor, with the usual round of fleet exercises, including gunnery exercises. The so-called fleet exercise of that year was in the Caribbean. We were in that area from something like January to April.

Q: Approximately how many destroyers were under that command, how many were operational in the Pacific?

Adm. H.: I couldn't give a categorical answer to that. I would suppose that there must have been somewhere in the neighborhood of twenty or thirty. I was not concerned directly with the administration of the destroyers, you understand, at that time. My command was the flagship, not the destroyers.

Q: You had to be concerned about the Admiral?

Adm. H.: The Admiral and his staff and the performance of the flagship, not the administration of the destroyer squadrons.

One interesting circumstance during that year was the fact that Admiral Sexton had on his staff at the time the young man who not very many years later was the expert that flew - the ordnance expert, who flew with the atomic bomb to Hiroshima. He was Admiral Sexton's staff gunnery officer.

Q: This was Parsons?

Adm. H.: Parsons, yes.

Q: Are there any particular demands placed upon the skipper of a ship that is a flagship? Over and above the ordinary?

Adm. H.: Well, of course, carrying the flag officer and his staff imposes certain special demands upon a flagship and the flagship personnel, including the skipper - perhaps especially the skipper.

Q: You mean in the spit-and-polish area?

Adm. H.: No, not necessarily because I don't think that spit and polish is very much more prevalent on flagships than it is on other ships in our service. Of course, there are certain extra duties that fall upon the personnel of a flagship compared to a ship that is not carrying a flag.

Q: Such as in the area of communications?

Adm. H.: Yes, that's one, and in the area of official traffic of various kinds. When you say "communications," you have in mind signals and radio and correspondence, etc? Yes, in addition to that, of course, a flagship is bound to have more official visitors than a ship that isn't carrying a flag, and it comes under more eyes, you might say.

Q: That's why I referred to the spit and polish. You want to be on your toes all the time, or you have to be?

Adm. H.: I suppose there is that factor.

Q: Is there ever any interference on the part of the flag officer with the skipper and his own immediate responsibilities?

Adm. H.: In my experience, no. Of course, the flagship like any other units of a flag officer's command is subject to his inspections et cetera and his general oversight, and, of course, the flagship comes more directly under the official eye than does a ship that is not a flagship in many ways.

Q: You speak about the extra visitors on board. Is there an extra allowance given to a flagship for entertaining such people at the mess? Do you have to absorb all of that?

Adm. H.: I don't recall that any extra burden of entertaining fell on us, really, if that's what you had in mind.

Q: Well, when you're in San Diego or some place like that and you have visitors on board you must show them some hospitality?

Adm. H.: Are you thinking of sightseeing visitors or more of official visitors?

Q: Exactly.

Adm. H.: Well, of course, official visitors add to the boat traffic at a flagship and the traffic of come and go across the gangway, so there is a little extra burden of that kind. And, perhaps, there's a tendency or incentive on board a flagship to pay more attention to spit and polish than other ships do, but I don't think that the discrepancy in that connection is very great because all the ships are subject to inspections with or without notice, on the part of the flag officer.

Q: Did your duty take you as far as Hawaii at all?

Adm. H.: In the Detroit?

Q: Yes.

Adm. H.: In the Detroit the only departure from the usual West Coast movements, I think, was the fleet problem, or fleet concentration rather, which was largely in the Caribbean, almost entirely in the Caribbean. It involved a transit of the Canal and it so happened the Canal transit was at night, and the Canal pilot after he took us through the locks on the west side at San Miguel and Miraflores he wished me luck and went below! So I was my own pilot through the Gatun Lake passage. I didn't see the pilot again until we arrived at the locks on the east side.

Q: Sounds like a very casual pilot!

Adm. H.: That may have been standard procedure with the Canal pilots, I don't know. That was the one time when I went through the Canal in a ship under my own command. That pilot apparently had confidence in the Navy being able to pilot their own ships through the Gatun Lake area, even at night.

Q: Or maybe in that particular skipper, he had confidence.

Adm. H.: I don't know. Anyhow, that was one occasion when I was up all night because I didn't leave the bridge that night.

Q: You didn't have any confidence in some of your under-officers?

Adm. H.: Well, it was not a matter of having confidence in them. Here was a special situation which I felt required my presence.

Q: That fleet exercise which took you into the Caribbean was certainly guaranteed not to provoke the Japanese in any way, was it not?

Adm. H.: I imagine so.

Q: Incidentally, did we engage in other operations in the Alaskan waters after the one in which you participated?

Adm. H.: Well, there were operations up there during World War II, you know.

Q: I know, but prior to World War II and after the one you engaged in?

Adm. H.: None that I know of.

Q: So maybe those protests were effective in that sense?

Adm. H.: As far as I'm aware that was the one time when a fleet problem involved the positioning of units in Alaskan or Aleutian waters. Whether that was just a happenstance, I don't know.

Q: There was an occasion while you were skipper of the Detroit when you did visit the Hawaiian Islands?

Adm. H.: Oh, yes, but we haven't come to that. That was after the fleet concentration in the Caribbean that I've just been talking about.

Q: I see.

Adm. H.: In our discourse, we haven't arrived at the point where we take the Detroit to Hawaii!

Q: All right, Sir. Just now, we're traversing the Panama Canal and we're doing it at night!

Adm. H.: We were just making our way through the Panama Canal when I had to stay up all night.

That was an incident. It rather took me by surprise because I had supposed that the pilot was on board for other reasons than just entering and leaving locks, but it appears that that was his responsibility and that was it. Getting from the Pacific locks to the Atlantic locks was my responsibility!

Q: In case something had happened during that transit, would the pilot have been blamed in any way?

Adm. H.: I can't answer that question categorically because I don't know enough about the Panama Canal regulations, but I admit that I was a little surprised. I would have expected to be on the bridge myself during the whole passage, but I'll admit that it was unexpected that I did the piloting from one end of the Gatun channels to the other.

Q: There was a certain degree of tension there that would not have been there if the pilot had been performing his duty?

Adm. H.: He may have been performing his duty. I don't mean to say that he was derelict because I don't know what his orders may have been and I don't know what the practice in the Panama Canal was at that time. What I'm saying is that I was surprised when the pilot turned the bridge back to me when we got out of the Pacific locks and then disappeared. I was capable of piloting the ship through Gatun Lake myself because the channels are well marked and it isn't a difficult proposition for one who knows his ship and has an adequate set of navigation aids, like lighted buoys and that sort of thing.

Well, that was an incident of our passage from the Pacific to the Atlantic for the strategic fleet problem that we had in the Caribbean that particular winter. I don't think there's much I can say about that set of problems. I don't remember too much about the problems themselves. I do remember a day when the Detroit had to refuel alongside an oiler, off Culebra Island, under rather difficult circumstances of wind and sea. That was another occasion when I had to be my own pilot putting the Detroit alongside the tanker. Of course, I didn't expect a pilot for that, but neither did I expect that there would be a fresh breeze blowing and the tanker at anchor tailing into the shore.

Q: Was this a fleet auxiliary, this tanker?

Adm. H.: Yes. I don't remember any other special incidents of that stay in the Caribbean. We wound up at Guantanamo and operated from there for a while.

When the fleet returned to the West Coast, the Detroit was detached immediately to go for an overhaul period at Pearl Harbor and I was relieved and detached at Pearl Harbor and ordered to the staff of the Commander-in-Chief. The Commander-in-Chief was still on the East Coast and I came up from Honolulu on a merchant liner. I was able to visit my family at Coronado for a day or so, and then on to the East Coast, and got there in time to go back to the Pacific with the fleet.

Q: Who was Commander-in-Chief? Was J. O. Richardson Commander-in-Chief then?

Adm. H.: C. C. Bloch was the Commander-in-Chief at that time. He was relieved later by J. O. Richardson, but at the time Admiral Richardson relieved Admiral Block I was detached and ordered East.

Q: It's very interesting, your constantly being assigned on the staff of the commander of a division or the commander-in-chief. I mean you got lots of staff duty, did you not?

Adm. H.: I had quite a bit of staff duty, yes.

Q: How do you account for that?

Adm. H.: Well, my first staff duty was during World War I and I account for that - I was ordered as flag secretary to the staff of Admiral A. F. Fechteler in 2 Battleship Division. I think that's been covered previously in our notes. And I think that the circumstance there was that my predecessor on Admiral Fechteler's staff was a classmate and friend of mine, Theodore Wilkinson. Wilkinson and I had both been given postgraduate courses in ordnance. That's been covered in our previous notes. After a period at sea, Wilkinson was due for shore duty and the Bureau of Ordnance wanted him, but Admiral Fechteler had to have a flag secretary, so I think that Wilkinson must have made a suggestion to Admiral Fechteler that he request that I be ordered as his flag secretary, I being in his division already. I think that's the way that happened.

I guess my next time was when I was ordered as the staff gunnery officer in the Battleship Division with Admiral Nulton. I think that maybe that was rather a natural one, too, because Admiral Nulton was coming in from ashore without a fleet staff and what he was doing actually was , I think, to request the senior gunnery officer in his outfit be ordered to his staff as the Battleship Divisions' gunnery officer, because I happened to be the senior gunnery officer in the outfit at that time. So I think that's the way that happened.

But at the point to which we have now arrived, when I left the Detroit and reported to Admiral Block as his fleet operations officer there were several factors there, I think, one of them being the fact that the Detroit, which I commanded, was entering a period of Navy Yard overhaul, that Admiral Bloch knew me. I had been with him when he was Chief of the Bureau of Ordnance. Also, he was the commandant at the Naval Gun Factory when I first went there. So he knew me and I guess he figured that with the Detroit going in for overhaul I was available. That's the only explanation that I can give for that.

Q: Of course, having served on a staff, one acquires a certain amount of experience as a staff officer.

Adm. H.: Yes, that was another factor, I would presume.

Q: I would think that would be very valuable to a commander, to select somebody who had staff experience. Doesn't it require a certain know-how that isn't ordinary with the line officer?

Adm. H.: I think quite possibly a staff officer, through the very nature of things, comes into contact with a number of seniors who become acquainted with him as a member of the staff in some organization where they have served such as a division or a class of ships or what-not.

When I went with Admiral Block, of course, he had known me for a considerable time back. First of all, in the Bureau of Ordnance.

Q: As you pointed out in a previous interview, when I cited the fact that you were named as a staff officer to Admiral Nulton also as an aide, you elaborated on the term "aide" and concluded that, yes, indeed, all staff officers who were also called "aides" had a closer relationship with the commander-in-chief. It's a personal relationship very often.

Adm. H.: Well, yes, that is true.

Mrs. H.: He was always the last person, it seemed to me, to leave the ship. I'd be there and wait and wait while one boatload would come after another, off they'd go, and I'd wait and wait. He'd be the last man to leave the ship, all the time.

Adm. H.: I'm a slow operator!

Mrs. H.: He's a thorough operator and he wouldn't leave the ship until the assignment or whatever they called it, was done.

Q: Well, I think maybe it was unfair of me to try to get you to admit that quality, but you added it, so thank you very much.

Interview No. 6 with Vice Admiral Olaf M. Hustvedt, U.S. Navy
(Retired)

Place: His residence in Washington, D.C.

Date: Tuesday afternoon, 5 March 1974

Subject: Biography

By: John T. Mason, Jr.

Q: Well, Sir, we had reached the year 1939 and you had just left the Detroit and were taking over a new job as operations officer on the staff of Admiral Block, who was Commander-in-Chief of the U.S. Fleet.

Adm. H.: That's correct. This was at the end of the fleet concentration in the Atlantic and the fleet problem in the Caribbean. I was detached or, rather the Detroit was detached from the fleet and proceeded to the Navy Yard at Pearl Harbor for an overhaul, which was due by calendar. As soon as I had delivered the ship at the Navy Yard in Pearl Harbor I was detached and proceeded east to report to Admiral Block, who was still on the East Coast with the fleet.

We went on around to our normal base of operations in the Pacific very shortly after that.

Q: What was his flagship?

Adm. H.: His flagship at that time was the Pennsylvania, the battleship Pennsylvania. She had been the battle fleet flagship for quite a few years.

The rest of that year, which was 1939 —

Q: And on into 1940.

Adm. H.: Running up to 1940, yes. Admiral Block left the fleet in January of 1940 and was succeeded by Admiral Richardson. I was with Admiral Block and his staff until that time. I think actually that was in December of 1939, not in January of 1940. At any rate, it was around the 1st of January 1940 when I was detached and Admiral Block was relieved by Admiral Richardson, and I was ordered to temporary duty in the Office of the Chief of Naval Operations in the Navy Department as a sort of filler-in of a few months before going to the War College.

Q: First, tell me about those eight months with the U.S. fleet.

Adm. H.: Those eight months were spent in carrying out a normal sort of operating year for the fleet, with the battleships based on San Pedro-Long Beach, as usual, and the destroyers on San Diego, and submarines on Hawaii.

Q: Only the submarines based on Hawaii?

Adm. H.: At that time only the submarines were based on Hawaii the year round. I'm not sure whether the Mine Squadron, which had based on Hawaii, was still operating out of Pearl Harbor or not. I don't remember definitely as to that. You may recall that I spent a couple of years there myself in the early twenties.

Q: I realize that, yes. Pearl Harbor in 1939 was quite different from what it had been in the twenties, was it not?

Adm. H.: I don't remember that I saw very much of Pearl Harbor in 1939. I was in there on the Detroit. That was in 1939, I think.

Q: But when you were on the Pennsylvania you were not there? You didn't go in to Pearl Harbor?

Adm. H.: No, the Pennsylvania didn't make Pearl Harbor at all during the time that I was attached to Admiral Block's staff, so the last time I was in Pearl Harbor before the war, I think, was when I was there with the Detroit I suppose in 1937, 1938, along in there.

Q: I thought herhaps the Admiral went in to Pearl Harbor as Commander-in-Chief.

What were your duties as the operational officer on his staff?

Adm. H.: In addition to being operations officer I was also functioning as assistant chief of staff, which was more or less what the term implies. The duties of the operations officer were largely related to administrative duties within the staff to a certain degree and primarily to preparation of schedules for the fleet operations and the issuance of orders relating to the routine fleet exercises that were carried out from month to month on a fairly regular schedule and rotating between exercises at sea and little periods of machinery overhaul and rest at the fleet bases. That sort of thing was going on in 1939 and 1940 when I was with Admiral Block. It was really, I suppose, one of the last periods of its kind - it was the next to last period of its kind, I should say - before the fleet had the onset of World War II, because, as you know, Admiral Richardson who succeeded Admiral Block in command of the battle fleet was in command practically up to the time of the attack on Pearl Harbor, having been relieved only a very short time before that by Admiral Kimmel.

That period in 1939-40 gets us pretty close to 1941.

Q: Was there an obvious growing tension within the fleet at the prospect of a conflict?

Adm. H.: I don't think that we in the fleet were really sitting on the edges of our chairs waiting for the storm to break. I think in common with most people in the country the attack on Pearl Harbor came as a surprise. Of course, we were aware, as the country was aware, that there were

Long Beach, as usual. My family was in Long Beach during that year up to the time I was detached.

Q: Were you able to spend very much time with them?

Adm. H.: Well, the fleet schedule was roughly a week of exercises at sea and a couple of weeks in port. That was about the normal rotation, unless it was broken by a big fleet problem which was largely a winter activity. My recollection is that my staff duties as operations officer didn't give me an awful lot of time with the family, except during weekends.

Q: Was Admiral Bloch a demanding kind of boss?

Adm. H.: I wouldn't characterize him as being "demanding." I would say that Admiral Bloch had his situation as commander-in-chief very much in hand and I think he probably felt that he had an experienced staff and that routine administration and the usual type of fleet employment, which of course was maintaining readiness, was pretty well in hand. I don't think he he showed any disposition to be excessively demanding. I think he felt, as near as I could tell, that his staff was on the job and capable of performing its functions so that he was not cracking the whip.

Q: Did you have time for any golf or anything of that sort?

Adm. H.: No, in those years I didn't have time for golf.

Q: What about the inclination for it?

Adm. H.: I had never become a fanatic golfer. No, I don't remember any real recreation during this particular period and, as a matter of fact, during this time with the fleet and during previous times with the fleet based there on Long Beach I had never had any time that I felt could be devoted to personal recreation or personal exercise because I saw little enough of my family as it was. If I got ashore for a weekend, Saturday afternoon till Monday morning, I was doing things with my family rather then setting out for a golf course. I think that just about answers that question, doesn't it?

Q: Yes. You were detached simultaneously with Admiral Bloch and you came back to Washington. You told me, off tape, that you drove back.

Adm. H.: Drove back by way of Florida. At that time I was ticketed for the next session of the War College at Newport and, of course, that was not going to begin until mid-summer and here I was back in Washington along about the middle of January. So I was attached temporarily to the office of the Chief of Naval Operations and did duty there from January until June, when I went up to Newport to get settled and ready to take off with the class entering the War College during that summer.

Q: What did you accomplish in Washington during those six

tensions, but of course I had left the fleet almost a year before the Pearl Harbor attack, so I can't express any first-hand opinion of what the atmosphere or attitude was in the fleet during early 1941 up to December, because I wasn't there.

Q: I've always had the feeling that the Navy especially was aware of the inevitability of a conflict in the Pacific?

Adm. H.: Well, you know, I can remember during the days when I was a midshipman, which was some thirty-odd years before the attack on Pearl Harbor, that there was a feeling that I believe was rather general, although not expressed, that we had to be on the lookout for difficulty with Japan in the Pacific. It was generally reco ized I think as a fact of international life for a generation or more. I don't think there was any question about that because I can remember even when I was a midshipman and this was not very many years after the war with Spain, people in this country were wondering what expansion Japan might be up to in a generation to come. I don't think there's much question of that. It seemed to be a matter of geography in those days more than anything else.

Q: What sort of fleet exercises did you engage in in the Pacific at this point, in 1939?

Adm. H.: There was a fleet problem in that year. I don't recall too many of the details. Looking back on it now, I would say that that particular year of 1939-40 was a more or less normal operating year in the fleet. The war in Europe, of course, had come on and that was of great interest, naturally, to all of us and that was bringing about changes in viewpoint pretty rapidly - that is, viewpoint as to what the current situation was and what the situation might portend. That's as near as I can express it, the attitude and condition that we were under in the fleet at that time.

Q: Was there any heightened interest shown by Washington? Did the Chief of Naval Operations visit the fleet at any time?

Adm. H.: Not that I can recall. I remember that during the year that I was in the Detroit the Chairman of the Senate Naval Committee visited San Diego at one time.

Q: Was that David Walsh?

Adm. H.: Yes, I think it was Senator Walsh.. I don't remember any Secretary of the Navy visit during those couple of years.

Q: Where was your family at this point? In Coronado?

Adm. H.: My family was in Coronado during the year that I was in the Detroit, the Detroit being based with the destroyers at San Diego, naturally, since the Detroit was the flagship of destroyer squadrons. But when I left the Detroit and went to Admiral Bloch's staff the family moved to Long Beach, not long after that because the battleships were based on San Pedro-

Long Beach, as usual. My family was in Long Beach during that year up to the time I was detached.

Q: Were you able to spend very much time with them?

Adm. H.: Well, the fleet schedule was roughly a week of exercises at sea and a couple of weeks in port. That was about the normal rotation, unless it was broken by a big fleet problem which was largely a winter activity. My recollection is that my staff duties as operations officer didn't give me an awful lot of time with the family, except during weekends.

Q: Was Admiral Bloch a demanding kind of boss?

Adm. H.: I wouldn't characterize him as being "demanding." I would say that Admiral Bloch had his situation as commander-in-chief very much in hand and I think he probably felt that he had an experienced staff and that routine administration and the usual type of fleet employment, which of course was maintaining readiness, was pretty well in hand. I don't think he he showed any disposition to be excessively demanding. I think he felt, as near as I could tell, that his staff was on the job and capable of performing its functions so that he was not cracking the whip.

Q: Did you have time for any golf or anything of that sort?

Adm. H.: No, in those years I didn't have time for golf.

Q: What about the inclination for it?

Adm. H.: I had never become a fanatic golfer. No, I don't remember any real recreation during this particular period and, as a matter of fact, during this time with the fleet and during previous times with the fleet based there on Long Beach I had never had any time that I felt could be devoted to personal recreation or personal exercise because I saw little enough of my family as it was. If I got ashore for a weekend, Saturday afternoon till Monday morning, I was doing things with my family rather then setting out for a golf course. I think that just about answers that question, doesn't it?

Q: Yes. You were detached simultaneously with Admiral Bloch and you came back to Washington. You told me, off tape, that you drove back.

Adm. H.: Drove back by way of Florida. At that time I was ticketed for the next session of the War College at Newport and, of course, that was not going to begin until mid-summer and here I was back in Washington along about the middle of January. So I was attached temporarily to the office of the Chief of Naval Operations and did duty there from January until June, when I went up to Newport to get settled and ready to take off with the class entering the War College during that summer.

Q: What did you accomplish in Washington during those six

months?

Adm. H.: was a sort of general factotum, I would say, in the office of the Chief of Naval Operations at that time.

Q: was Admiral Stark, was it?

H.: Yes. I can't say that I look back upon any particular accomplishment. I was not there on a permanent enough basis to be assigned charge of a division of the office. I had been there in charge of the Central Division during my last preceding shore duty, but during this interim I was assigned office space but my duties were more or less as assigned and I've forgotten any special area of responsibility during those three or four months that I was there. I don't think it would have been logical to have placed me in charge of a division unless there was an actual division vacancy at that time, which there was not.

Q: Did you bring your children back to Washington?

Adm. H.: At that time, our daughter had been married for several years. Our elder son was a student at MIT, and the younger one was a boarder at St. Alban's School in Washington. So there wasn't very much question as to what the children were going to do!

Q: Did you look forward to this assignment at the Naval War College?

Adm. H.: Oh, yes. We all recognized, I think, in the line of the Navy that taking the line course at the Naval War College was almost a requirement for advancing in rank. I wouldn't say that it was so in an absolute sense, I think most line officers of that time were pretty well of the opinion that getting a War College course was almost must before one got out of the captain's grade.

Q: You were a captain at this point?

Adm. H.: I was a captain, yes.

Q: So you went into the senior class up at the War College?

Adm. H.: Yes, I went into the War College senior class. That instruction year at the War College began, as usual, around the 1st of July and in the latter part of that calendar year or quite soon after the turn of the year, in January or so, I was ordered detached from the War College to the Navy Yard in New York in connection with fitting out and commissioning the North Carolina.

Q: So you weren't permitted to have a full year there?

Adm. H.: No, I did not have a full year at the War College. Admiral Kalbfus, who was the president of the War College at that time, told me that I would be given due credits for my time at the War College and that he did want me to submit a thesis, which I accordingly did. I think I wrote my thesis largely during the period when we were commissioning the North Carolina.

Q: What was your thesis about?

Adm. H.: I'm afraid I would have to dig into some papers to see if I could find that thesis at this point, which of course is largely because that time in 1941 is now thirty-three years ago. I find it a little bit hard to remember the exact theme of that thesis because I don't think I've had occasion to review it at any time since then! I don't believe I could find it now, although no doubt it's in the house somewhere.

Q: Tell me a little about life at the Naval War College when you were there.

Adm. H.: As you're probably aware, the Naval War College does not go in for campus life. Nobody lives on the campus, except the president of the Naval War College and his immediate staff, his aides. I'm reminded of a quotation that's attributed to a head of MIT long ago, who was quoted as saying that MIT is a place for men to work and not for boys to play. I think that was distinctly the case with the War College in the days when I was a student officer because I don't remember any particular play associated with the "campus" at the War College.

Q: You do imply, then, that the course of studies was a fairly stiff one?

Adm. H.: It was to the extent that it required serious attendance, it required a schedule which made use of every day except for a normal weekend off. The atmosphere was one of serious pursuit of the objective and, of course, the people attached to the War College during their off hours saw something of each other and had a reasonable kind of social and recreational life. I don't mean to imply that the atmosphere at the War College was monastic or anything of that kind, but the War College life as a student officer was a serious type of existence. It wasn't a period of gaiety. I would suppose that that has been the atmosphere at the Naval War College right from the beginning.

Q: Where did you live? In town?

Adm. H.: We lived in town, at 18 1/2 Greenough Place.

Q: Did you find it an advantage for the balance of your naval career to have associated so closely with the various men there? Various naval officers who were in attendance as students also?

Adm. H.: That's a question I find a little difficult to answer. I have to run over in my mind, if I understand your question correctly, just who the people were. I don't remember anything special in that connection.

Q: Did you have any State Department people as students there?

Adm. H.: Not in the senior War College class at that time. As I remember it, the only student officers who were in the senior class during the period that I was there were naval officers, mostly of the line, and a few Marine officers. I don't remember any others.

Q: Were any foreign navies represented?

Adm. H.: No, not at that time. I've no doubt they have been since. But at that time, in 1940-41, no. There were several Marine officers in the class that I was in. I don't remember any other staff officers and there were none attached to the instruction staff that I can recall. Of course, we had a number of lecturers -

Q: You mean imported for the occasion?

Adm. H.: Yes - who appeared either for a single lecture or perhaps for two or three lectures during the course of the year, but I don't remember any staff officers in the student class while I was there. There were, as I say, at least a couple of Marine officers.

Q: Admiral Kalbfus was busy writing a book, was he not, at that point?

Adm. H.: I couldn't tell you. If he was, I wasn't aware of it. He may very well have been.

Q: How prominent were war games in the course of study?

Adm. H.: Oh, they played quite an important part. Even though I left the class early, I can recall that we had a number of games on the game board during the time I was there. I remember that one of the games that we had while I was there had to do with a problem that was set up in the Pacific, in which Truk was quite important as a geographical point. A couple of years later I was in the Pacific when the attack on the Marshall Islands took place, and when we attacked Truk and during the progress of that operation against the area - and it was going to be at that moment centered on Truk - the battleships in which I had a command at that time met up with the cruisers of the then fleet for the first time. I remember that that brought Admiral Ike Giffen and me together for the first time since we had been neighbors at the War College, and I recall that after the immediate fracas around Truk was over and we were going about our next movement I had time to send a little PVT, private message, to Admiral Giffen in his flagship. I said something to the effect, "How are you, Ike? It's great to meet up again on the old campus," because here we were actually operating around Truk which we had done on the game board at the War College a year or two before!

Q: That leads me to a question. A course at the War College should be of very great value then to a man in his career?

Adm. H.: It was certainly so regarded.

Hustvedt #6 - 187

Q: And actually so in your case?

Adm. H.: Actually I'm sure it was.

Q: You must have been rather reluctant to break off and leave the War College before the year was up?

Adm. H.: Well, that cut both ways. Certainly, I would not have thought of saying "oh, please let me stay at the War College, I don't want to command the North Carolina"!

Q: No. That was really a feather in your cap, was it not?

Adm. H.: I would suppose so, yes, she being the first battleship we had commissioned in a good many years.

Q: In sixteen years, was it not?

Adm. H.: I guess it was something like that.

Q: How did you happen to be selected for that command?

Adm. H.: I was of the right group in age and experience. Of course, when I say that I immediately have to recall that within a matter of two or three years the North Carolina was commanded successively by men who weren't out of high school at the time I went to the Naval Academy, or weren't out of high school at the time I was graduated from the Naval Academy, I guess.

Q: Yes, but war made a difference, didn't it?

Adm. H.: Yes.

Q: You were taking over in a time of still what you might call peace.. She was building in Brooklyn Navy Yard?

Adm. H.: Yes. Incidentally, a propos of what I have just said, I was by long odds the oldest commanding officer that the North Carolina had. I was succeeded by Oscar Badger, who is I think at least four years younger than I, and he was succeeded by someone younger, and so on down until before the war was over I think the North Carolina was commanded by skippers who were at least ten years my junior.

Q: I notice, however, that most of them had the same length of tenure as you.

Adm. H.: In command of her?

Q: Yes.

Adm. H.: Well, of course, in wartime those commands changed very quickly. I suppose actually it was because of the necessity for promoting people to take over new commands as they were organized.

Q: Of the nine commanding officers, only one had a tour of duty as skipper that was longer than a year, and he was in peacetime.

Adm. H.: The Navy was expanding steadily throughout the war, and I guess that's the only comment that one can make on that. Expansion means new commands and new commands mean that people with experience have got to be grabbed from here and there to fit into the new commands that are established.

Q: Your command of the North Carolina had added interest in that you prepared her for commissioning. Tell me about that phase of it.

Adm. H.: From the standpoint of the commanding-officer-to-be, that was largely a matter of organizing the crew and training them as they were assembled. The ship herself under construction, of course, is still in the hands of the Navy Yard and, although a crew, including both officers and men, is assembled and moved into the ship and takes a certain part in preparing the ship for commissioning, the ship is still under the jurisdiction of the Navy Yard authorities, from the commandant down, until she is actually placed into commission in the command of the designated commanding officer. So the yard period of preparation for commissioning is really a period of gradually turning a hulk into an operating unit and the personnel who were to be a part of that operating unit are assembled fairly early. They're not assembled full-blown as an organization. They're assembled somewhat gradually, you might say, and gradually fill up the spaces and the billets and become accustomed to the ship before they actually go aboard and make it their home and their job. It's a process that can't be accomplished overnight. I don't know just when the personnel that eventually manned the North Carolina first began to be assembled at the Navy Yard in the so-called receiving ship, and I don't recall exactly what percentage of the crew we had at the time the ship was actually commissioned. I suppose that we had somewhere in the neighborhood of perhaps two-thirds of the crew at the moment the ship was commissioned.

Q: What was her complement?

Adm. H.: Oh, the eventual complement of the North Carolina was somewhere in the neighborhood of 2,700 to 3,000 men, officers and men.

Q: I would assume that as the men assembled there many of them were new recruits to the Navy, were they?

Adm. H.: A good many were but, of course, there had to be a pretty strong, not nucleus, but framework of men with experience.

Q: Did you have a strong voice in the selection of your officers?

Adm. H.: No, I had almost none. When I say that I don't mean to intimate that I tried to have a voice and was denied. I simply chose not to attempt to exercise a voice.

Q: You were willing to take whomever the Bureau of Personnel sent you?

Adm. H.: Yes. On that account, I don't know to what extent a prospective commanding officer can presume to exercise a voice, and I don't know simply because I never tested it.

Q: That's in terms of personnel. What happened in terms of ordnance, for instance? You were very close to the ship and knew what was being installed. Did you have any occasion to say "I would like something different?"

Adm. H.: Before the ship was commissioned? The ship was commissioned in early April of 1941. I appeared on the scene in approximately in the middle of February. I was there about six weeks before the ship was commissioned. It's fairly obvious that I could have very little voice about what went into the ship in the way of material, or personnel for that matter.

Q: The men were sent to various schools, were they?

Adm. H.: Yes, some of them had been at trade schools, a good many of them were men who were beyond their first enlistment. In other words, a great many of them were already petty officers, including chief petty officers. I have never served in the Bureau of Personnel, so I'm not too much acquainted with the processes whereby the Bureau of Personnel assembles a crew to man a new ship. It's something that I have, you might say, an academic acquaintance with, but no close personal acquaintance through having gone through the actual assembly process myself.

Q: Did you as a prospective skipper have to brush up on shiphandling or anything of the sort?

Adm. H.: No, I don't remember that that entered into the picture with me. I had been a shiphandler to some extent as a watch officer in battleships, as executive officer in a heavy cruiser - I did a good deal of shiphandling as executive officer, and again as commanding officer of the Detroit. I don't remember that there was any way in which I could prepare for shiphandling in the North Carolina beyond what I already knew. As a matter of fact, this was the first time I had known that any prospective commanding officers were given a preparatory course.

*Q: That's what he told me happened to him, and he took command of the New Jersey before Korea. It was just before Korea because the New Jersey participated in Korean action. I was going to ask you, the North Carolina was equipped with radar, was she?

Adm. H.: Yes.

Q: This required special instruction of some of your crew, did it not?

Adm. H.: It doesn't require any special instruction particularly, I think, of a commanding officer who is going to enjoy the

*NOTE: An off the tape reference to a commanding officer of the BB New Jersey.

benefits of the information that is gained by radar, because the commanding officer doesn't have to be a radar expert.

Q: No, but you had certain personnel on board who were experts?

Adm. H.: Oh, yes, certainly.

Q: And they had to be specially trained for this job?

Adm. H.: Yes, that's true.

Q: What kind of radar was installed on the North Carolina?

Adm. H.: I'm not sure that I understand that question fully. The radar of the then state of the art, I'm sure, was installed in the North Carolina, including a radarscope in the pilothouse and a radarscope in plot. Just where else I'm not sure.

Q: Was it the installation they called the "bedspring," that huge installation?

Adm. H.: The antenna array that we had in the North Carolina had advanced somewhat beyond the bedspring. The first antennae that appeared in the fleet were distinctly of the bedspring type.

Interview No. 7 with Vice Admiral Olaf M. Hustvedt, U.S. Navy
(Retired)

Place: His residence in Washington, D.C.

Date: Tuesday afternoon, 26 March 1974

Subject: Biography

By: John T. Mason, Jr.

Q: It's a delight to see you on this spring day and see you looking so chipper.

Adm. H.: You brought nice weather with you!

Q: Today, we are to have the story of the North Carolina, the battleship - your command of her, and I think perhaps it's appropriate at this point for you to tell me the story of her second name, the "Showboat."

Adm. H.: That is easily told. I can't give any dates connected with it, but I think I can give you an authentic version and authentic versions are few and far between because the crew of the North Carolina got out a little weekly news sheet during the time she was in commission, except I suppose during the war years, and I have seen in that news sheet a supposed account of the origin of the pet name which was totally erroneous. I can I think give the authentic version.

I believe we already have on tape the fact that the North Carolina and Washington made their shake-down cruise in company. They joined up for that shake-down cruise at Hampton Roads, each of them coming from the building yards, the North Carolina from the Navy Yard, New York, and the Washington from the Navy Yard, Philadelphia. The North Carolina was at the Hampton Roads anchorage first, and I chose to anchor upstream. The Washington, when she came in, was a normal distance downstream, I suppose the usual 500 yards or so, and we were just above Old Point.

The day before we started on the cruise I called a conference consisting of the two skippers, Captain Benson and myself, and the two executive officers to settle some of the items of collaboration that needed to be gone into before we put to sea together bound for Guantanamo. When that conference broke up, or was about to break up, the executive officer of the Washington made reference in a joking way to something that was news to me and I think was news to my executive officer, Commander Shepard. He said that the men on the Washington had taken to calling the North Carolina "Showboat." Of course, it was well understood, I think, among all of us without going very deeply into the subject that the men in the Washington were considering the North Carolina a showboat because she was getting a great, great deal of attention at that time in the metropolitan daily press. Not only the daily press, but we were in the New Yorker with a small item. We were on the radio in connection with the commissioning, and so on. In other words, the North Carolina had been getting a great deal of publicity.

Q: Partly because she was the first battleship in sixteen years?

Adm. H.: Yes. Well, of course, the Washington was on our heels. She was just as respectable a ship and had been commissioned within a month or two of our commissioning. But I think the difference was that the North Carolina during her commissioning ceremonies and during her fitting-out some little while afterwards, operating out of the New York Navy Yard had been very much in the press, and I make no doubt that the men on the Washington were feeling a little bit left out. Anyhow, we were told that the Washington men were fond of referring to the North Carolina as "the showboat," or "that showboat," perhaps.

Later on that day or possibly the next morning when I was talking to Commander Shepard our executive officer, about getting under way et cetera, I told him that I wanted the crew at quarters as for a formal inspection and that the usual passing honors would be exchanged when we would go by the Washington at her position. She was going to follow us out of the harbor –

Q: Seniority!

Adm. H.: – and on the spur of the moment I said to Commander

Shepherd, "Incidentally, referring to what we heard yesterday about the relations between the crews, I think that after the exchange of formal honors, the 'Star-Spangled Banner' and so on, I want the band to play 'Here comes the showboat,'" which duly was done the following day and I think that was a clincher, in a way, with the crew of the North Carolina because I think they must have been hearing the scuttlebutt about our name on board the Washington. I think the men thought that was a fine business, our bursting forth with "Here comes the showboat" the first time we passed the Washington. As it so happened, the nickname stuck not only with the men of the Washington but the men of the North Carolina, they adopted the idea immediately and it wasn't long, as I remember it, before - no, I don't think the name of our little weekly publication, which was called The Tarheel, was ever changed, but there was a sort of memorial book published in honor of the ship not very many years afterward, which they titled The Showboat. I think there's no question that the men on the North Carolina took to the name like ducks to water and the ship was thereafter "the showboat."

That's the story.

Q: A delightful story.

Well, Sir, after her trial run you were in business. Tell me about your command of the ship.

Adm. H.: We had just started on our shake-down cruise, which was not particularly eventful. I suppose shake-down cruises are regularly uneventful. One break we had in the North Carolina was that I asked for and got permission from the Navy Department to take the ship to Kingston, Jamaica, for a weekend during our shake-down period, that in order to give the crew a little break. That visit to Kingston was uneventful. I scarcely left the ship, although I did naturally pay my respects to the Governor General. The crew was allowed some liberty. Otherwise, it was just a pleasant weekend. It was a new place to look at and some very fine summer weather. It was summertime but, as I remember it, Jamaica was not specially hot, getting some advantage from trade winds and that sort of thing.

After completing our stay at Guantanamo for drills of various kinds, we and the Washington departed in company bound for our respective home yards, but on the way, off the Delaware Capes, we had an opportunity to exercise our antiaircraft batteries against sleeve targets towed by planes from the Naval Air Station, Cape May. I think we had an air station there at that time.

Q: Yes, we did.

Adm. H.: The scene of that firing was offshore from Cape May. It was, incidentally, quite a revelation to see what could be accomplished in the way of hitting a towed target with the then new categories of antiaircraft batteries that new battleships had, from the 5-inch, double-purpose guns to the antiaircraft machine guns of various calibers. The practice on the whole was very satisfactory in that regard.

Then we returned to our home bases and the process of completing the fitting-out and organizing and drilling the crews went on from there.

Later on, we had a period for more drills at sea that were conducted in the Chesapeake Bay, including the so-called de-gaussing of the ship on a range that had been established in Chesapeake Bay, not far from the drill grounds that we normally used in the Tangier Sound vicinity.

It was while we were on those drill grounds and while we were at anchor overnight that we received the report of the selections of th- current selection board which had just finished its deliberations in Washington, and I learned that I had been selected for promotion to flag rank. That, as I remember it, was rather late in August.

After that, opportunity to do some real drill with the crew, we returned to Navy Yard, New York, for completion of our outfitting, which involved naturally a multiplicity of small details of testing, and equipping, and stores of various kinds. We were still at the Navy Yard, New York, when orders for my detachment came along around, as I remember it, late October or early November, and I then proceeded to Newport to report to Commander-in-Chief, Atlantic Fleet, then Vice Admiral E. J. King on board his flagship Augusta, for duty as his Chief of Staff.

Q: May I ask you a question or two about the North Carolina? This must have been an occasion of joy to be elevated to flag rank but also a sad occasion to have such a short period of command of her?

Adm. H.: Yes, there were disappointments connected with that, especially in view of the fact that my first months in the chief-of-staff billet were spent not at sea but in the old Constellation alongside the pier at the Training Station, Newport. So I was going from one sea billet to another, but the second sea billet was at that time virtually a shore billet and remained so until quite a few months later when the Vixen was taken over as flagship for the Commander-in-Chief, Atlantic. But that's getting ahead of the story.

Q: Yes. Tell me, Sir, about the exercises in Chesapeake Bay. This was the general practice, was it?

Adm. H.: Well, of course, the exercises that we could perform in Chesapeake Bay were fairly limited, but one of the principal reasons, I think, for that period in Chesapeake Bay was the de-gaussing of the ship. Did I mention that?

Q: You just mentioned it in passing, that she was de-gaussed.

Adm. H.: There was a de-gaussing range somewhere in the vicinity of Tangier Sound, and it was just off that de-gaussing range, I believe, that we were anchored for the night when I got the word that I'd been selected.

Q: But, as you say, the waters of the Chesapeake Bay were somewhat limiting in what you could do in the way of exercising.

Adm. H.: Oh, yes, there isn't much you can do in Chesapeake Bay. As I remember it, a certain amount of small-caliber firing can be done there. Turret-firing pretty well necessitates going off into deep water, such as outside the bay, off the Virginia Capes. So the actual training exercises in Chesapeake Bay were, you might say, minimal.

Q: Did the wartime situation which pertained as far as Europe was concerned, was this one of the reasons for exercising in the bay?

Adm. H.: No, I don't think so really. I presume that the availability of the secure and secluded anchorage was one factor. I can't recall definitely whether our gun-firing trials which were held off the Newfoundland Banks came at just about that period or a little bit earlier. I'm not sure of my dates in that regard. We haven't covered them, have we?

Q: No.

Adm. H.: Well, that's a part of this same period and perhaps we might as well mention that now.

Like other new ships, or at least new major ships, the North Carolina was put through gunfire trials, tests, which were actually a test of the gun mounts and other accessories. The guns themselves, of course, had gone through proving ground proofs, so they had been fired previously. The gun-firing trials were to test everything, including foundations and the like.

In line with the considerable degree of public interest that the North Carolina had occasioned, especially, as I say, under the guns of the New York press, arrangements were made for press representatives to board the ship for the period of the gun trials and we had on board I suppose around two dozen press representatives, including some rather famous names. I hesitate to name them because I don't wish to discriminate by leaving anyone out!

Q: I'll bet Hanson Baldwin was one of them?

Adm. H.: Hanson Baldwin was one, yes, and there were others whose names are, or were then, familiar to every newspaper reader.

Q: Walter Winchell was one of the other correspondents, but if we get the list we'll add it at the end.

Tell me what were they interested in on board ship and what did you have to do?

Adm. H.: They were interested in everything. As a matter of fact, I saw very little of those correspondents, except seeing them as they made their way around, because under the circumstances I was on the bridge practically from the time we left port until we came back into port, sleeping in my sea cabin, which was just off the bridge. I think I almost didn't get off the bridge except towards the end of the period, after we had had our gun-firing trials et cetera and, as I remember it, on the way back to port I invited the correspondents to come to my cabin for a cup of coffee. We had a little gathering there with some items for discussion for an hour or so. That was my only real personal contact with those press people, because under the circumstances I was fairly well confined to the bridge as long as specific activities were going on. But we tried to make the period at sea as short as possible consistent with making all the tests that we were supposed to make.

Q: Were these men limited in what they could print about the North Carolina?

Adm. H.: I think that they were required, although I'm not sure, to submit their copy to a form of censorship which was actually exercised by a representative of the Commander, Third Naval District, under whose authority the ship was at the time. The ship had not joined a fleet, you understand. She was still undergoing fitting-out in some respects at the Navy Yard, New York, so that she was technically under the wing of the naval district commander, who at that time was Admiral Adolphus Andrews. It's my recollection that the naval district commander had a representative on board who was sort of a guide, counselor, and friend to the gentlemen of the press and was also an authority through which their copy passed, as long as they were on the ship. That's my recollection. The matter of press was really not in my own official hands so much as it was in the hands of the naval district commander.

Q: This was in the period of the so-called armed neutrality, consequently you had to be rather observant of possible enemy craft?

Adm. H.: Yes. Of course, that was a period in which German submarines were actually operating in waters of the Western Atlantic. I would not attempt to say, because I can't recollect definitely, how close there had been submarine attacks. Of course, there would have been absolutely no justification for attacking the North Carolina, except as an act of war. But I think the country was very sensitive to the matter of submarines operating in the Western Atlantic and I think the gentlemen of the press on board had German submarine operations very much on their minds, not that they were fearful of our being attacked but I think they perhaps were just wondering whether there might not be a sight or sound contact with German submarines in the waters that we were entering, which actually was more or less off the banks of Newfoundland, or at least projecting up into that area. So we were within not too many miles of belligerent coasts, the coast of Canada. Canada was actually at war alongside the rest of the empire, so that German submarines were rather obviously on the minds of some of the gentlemen of the press. I remember that there were certain comments on the subject during that little session that I had with them in my cabin over coffee and cakes.

Q: Tell me about the gunnery trials. Were they successful? Were you able to complete them in a short period of time?

Adm. H.: Yes, the gun trials went off very smoothly and nothing untoward developed. Some of the firing involving the antiaircraft battery, which was also our torpedo defense battery, was conducted at night.

I'm reminded of the fact that I was given permission to have my younger son on board with me for that particular small period at sea, which I think perhaps I would not have requested except for the fact that we had a very large group of civilians on board anyhow in the persons of the press. I had my son, Stephen, with me. He at that time was seventeen years old, still a prep school boy, and without making an issue of it the gunnery officer had allowed my son to press the button for one of the salvoes which, of course, was an experience that he has never forgotten.

Q: I expect the guns on the North Carolina and her gun power, so to speak, stood out in contrast with what you had first known on the West Virginia and then the Oklahoma back in the teens?

Adm. H.: Yes. Of course, there was a difference in degree. I think sofar as guns were concerned the striking thing in my mind at the time was the versatility of the secondary battery, combined torpedo defense and antiaircraft 5-inch guns, because the turrets themselves were the latest and biggest. Seeing those turrets fired was much like seeing other turrets within my experience fired, but the antiaircraft battery was something else. We'd never had anything like that aboard ship before.

Q: At that point, you were equipped with radar also?

Adm. H.: Oh, yes. Radar had been in the fleet for some years because I can remember very distinctly radar in the fleet the last time I had taken part in a fleet concentration in the Caribbean, which must have been at least two or three years before that.

Q: Did Admiral King come on board the North Carolina?

Adm. H.: He was on board for the commissioning. I don't remember that he was on board again during the period of my command. Admiral King's headquarters along about that time were in Newport aboard the old Constellation, and he probably wouldn't have had occasion to visit the North Carolina again after she was commissioned unless he chose to do so at the Navy Yard, New York.

Q: Did Secretary Knox come on board ever?

Adm. H.: Secretary Knox was on board for the commissioning, so was Mayor La Guardia of New York City. Governor Bolton of North Carolina was on board for the commissioning.

Q: As the showboat, you must have had a lot of VIPs in those days before we actually got into war?

Adm. H.: Yes, there were a good many people who had an interest in the ship. Among them were Junius Morgan and his wife. We became quite well acquainted with them as a direct result of my being there in New York in command of the North Carolina. Junius Morgan at that time, I believe - I'm almost certain - was an officer in the Naval Reserve, even before we entered the war, and the Junius Morgans presented to the ship after she was commissioned a triptych for the altar. When it came to equipping the "church" on board, the official funds, if any, were extremely limited. The altar equipment was largely donated by, as I've already mentioned, the Junius Morgans and by my wife's brother, Mr. Alfred D. Cooper, who was at that time a resident of the Philippines and had been for many, many years.

Q: How large a chapel did she have?

Adm. H.: The ship had no chapel. Church was rigged in a selected compartment below decks and in a selected location above decks for good weather. But there was no chapel as such. I think we have some pictures here which will show the chapel rig.

Q: You said off tape that you had an organ on board.

Adm. H.: Yes. To complete remarks about the equipping of the chapel, perhaps the most important item was an organ which was donated by Mrs. Unger Vetleson. Her son was one of the Reserve ensigns attached to the ship at the time of commissioning, which explains her interest, and that son a year or two later became my flag lieutenant for a period.

Q: I take it you must have had a chaplain on board, too?

Adm. H.: Yes. All Navy ships of that date had chaplains. I think all battleships and major aircraft carriers had chaplains attached, and it wasn't long after commissioning when church services were held on board regularly, rain or shine, because we had arrangements whereby we set up chapel below decks if above decks didn't come up with good weather.

Q: How did the ship handle, Sir? Did she come up to your expectations and those of the Bureau of Ships?

Adm. H.: I don't remember any special comments from the Bureau. As far as I was personally concerned, I think her handling qualities were excellent. Of course, like all major ships, the handling at close quarters except in emergencies at sea means normally that the ship has a pilot on board. For instance, going into and out of the New York Navy Yard, we always had a pilot on board from the berth at the Navy Yard down to somewhere in the vicinity of Tompkinsville. I think the pilot normally came out from Tompkinsville and we normally dropped him at Tompkinsville because in and out of New York I think we normally had a pilot who was attached to New York Navy Yard, although he naturally had to be a member of the Pilots' Association and a qualified pilot for New York harbor. The one that we normally had was, I think, actually attached to the Navy Yard itself.

Q: The North Carolina actually joined the fleet while you were still in command, did she not?

Adm. H.: No, because after the gun trials and the shake-down cruise we returned to the Navy Yard and proceeded with the matter of fitting-out, as it's called, and we were still in that fitting-out category at the time I was relieved of command, which, as I recollect it, was late in October.

Q: She was intended for service with the Atlantic Fleet, was she?

Adm. H.: No, I wouldn't say that she was intended for service with the Atlantic Fleet. I'd say that she was intended, if you can speak of her being intended, for service wherever the battleship squadrons were operating, and they had been operating mostly in the Pacific for a number of years.

Q: Admiral, tell me something about some of the social life

which involved you and Mrs. Hustvedt when the North Carolina, as the newest battleship, was berthed in New York.

Adm. H.: I think it has already appeared in this account that the North CArolina excited a great deal of interest in the press and, therefore, presumably in the public, and a good deal of interest among our neighbors in New York City just gene-ally speaking. For instance, I recall that one of the events during our Navy Yard stay, and as I remember it, it was towards the end of the time that I was in the ship, a group of Latin American chiefs of naval establishments convened in Washington for an official conference - I presume, naturally, at the invitation of our president. And during the course of their visit to this country, they came in a body to New York and, I presume, inspected the Navy Yard and in connection with their visit I was requested by the local naval authorities to entertain them at luncheon on board the North Carolina, which I accordingly did. That, of course, attracted a great deal of press attention and there were representatives of the press on the outskirts there. As a part of the proceedings of that day, the luncheon on the North Carolina was followed by a cruise around Manhattan Island aboard Vincent Astor's yacht. My wife and and I were invited to be a part of the official party on this Nourmahal cruise, which was a very pleasant occasion.

It has already been mentioned here, I think, that among

the civilian guests on the Nourmahal on that occasion were Katherine Hepburn and Brenda Fraser, the then reigning debutantes of New York City, both of whom were very well publicized figures, and, of course, the press and cameramen were on board the Nourmahal too. I happened to hear in passing one of the press photographers say to another, "Let's get the Number One skipper and the Number One debutante." I made up my mind that I wasn't going to be a party to that, if I could gracefully avoid it, so I made myself active in circulating for a while so that the photographers wouldn't be able to corner me very easily!

After the cruise around Manhattan, the Nourmahal was secured at one of the piers way up town and the party was met there by a fleet of, I don't suppose they were taxicabs, maybe some of them were, anyhow a fleet of limousines or something of the sort which took us down Fifth Avenue to the residence of Mrs. Cornelius Vanderbilt, where the whole official party had been invited to stop in and have tea. Mrs. Vanderbilt was very cordial, as I presume she was by habit, and I recall that, in speaking to my wife and me, she invited us to, in effect, drop in when we could.

The presence of the ship in New York and the vast amount of publicity that attended her movements at that time really, apparently, caused a widespread interest in the area and my wife and I were invited for various occasions for varying periods by several people whose names were very well known.

Among the people with whom we became very well acquainted was the mother of one of our young Reserve officers attached to the ship, whose name was Monell. He was a son of Ambrose Monell of Monell Metal fame. His mother, after, I believe, a good many years of widowhood had remarried and she married a gentleman whose name was Unger Vetleson, of Norwegian birth. The Vetlesons were very cordial in their invitations to us and we spent, I think, during the course of the summer a couple of weekends with them at their place on Long Island.

Q: When you left the North Carolina to assume your duties of flag rank, I understand that they gave you a going-away party on board ship?

Adm. H.: Yes, that was a very large affair and in the course of it I was presented with going-away gifts from the officers and crew in the shape of a very handsome silver bowl, I think of the type called a REvere bowl, isn't it, that one?

Q: Yes.

Adm. H.: Plus my flag officer shoulder marks and a uniform cap. That was a large and successful party.

Q: That was held in New York?

Adm. H.: That was given at the St. George Hotel in Brooklyn, as I remember it.

Q: Well, that was a very nice thing to do, a very touching thing, I would imagine?

Adm. H.: Yes, especially since I had been skipper to that collection of personnel for not very much more than six months. Well, including the preliminary fitting-out period before commissioning, I suppose it was closer to eight months.

Q: That says that you must have made a real impact on them.

Adm. H.: I would be at a loss to assess that statement! Presumably, I left with no ill will from anyone on board, as far as I know.

Q: However, you stayed in contact with the North Carolina?

Adm. H.: Since then?

Q: Yes.

Adm. H.: I had a number of subsequent contacts with the ship, but as I recall it, when I left the ship in the late fall of 1941, I think I didn't see her again until in the far Pacific in 1944, because my duties as chief of staff to the Commander-in-Chief, Atlantic, took me immediately to Newport. Then, when the Augusta was detached from duty as flagship to the Commander-in-Chief, Atlantic, the flag office and headquarters, including the Admiral and his staff, were moved to the old Constellation at her permanent berth at the Training Station in

Newport, and the Constellation was quickly fitted up with the necessary offices and communications and other necessities to serve as the command post for the Commander-in-Chief, Atlantic.

The Augusta was still being used to some extent, as I remember it, until the ex-yacht Vixen was acquired and provided with offices and quarters and communications outlets, so that she could serve as a somewhat mobile flagship, which she did from thence onward, I think throughout the course of the war.

Q: To resume the story of your contact with the North Carolina in after years, you told me recently you did see her in the Pacific in 1944. Do you want to take up the story at that point?

Adm. H.: I suppose you know - many people, perhaps, do not - that during the war operations in the Pacific, actual personal communications from ship to ship, which is commonplace in peacetime, almost disappear. That is partly because people are a lot busier. There isn't much time for any visiting around that isn't related to the war effort. Also the fact that in wartime combatant ships are strict about everything that can be disposed of as being non-essential and especially anything that is a fire hazard, combustible. The consequence is that during war operations the number of boats that are carried by combatant ships are reduced to a minimum. That curtails ship visiting until it almost disappears.

After I left the North Carolina in New York in the late autumn of 1941, I don't recall seeing her again until I joined the forces operating in the far Pacific in January of 1944. Then I found myself operating for a good part of the year 1944 in the same formation with the North CArolina, but I never had the opportunity or occasion for going on board the North Carolina until quite a few years later, after she had become a relic in a museum at Wilmington, North Carolina.

Q: You went down for the official opening of her as a museum?

Adm. H.: Yes, I was present at the official opening of the so-called USS North Carolina Battleship Memorial in Wilmington.

Q: Is your voice preserved there on tape on board the battleship?

Adm. H.: Not that I know of. I don't recall that back around 1941 we did a great deal of recording on tape. I can recall that it had come into use a very few years later, into rather general use. I'm not talking about the fleet, I'm talking about civilian life, because I know that my son, to whom I have already referred, when he finally got to college, which was after serving during the war, used tapes in connection with his college studies, and that was about in 1947 or so.

Interview No. 8 with Vice Admiral Olaf M. Hustvedt, U.S. Navy
(Retired)

Place: His residence in Washington, D.C.

Date: Wednesday afternoon, 17 April 1974

Subject: Biography

By: John T. Mason, Jr.

Q: It's great to see you on this beautiful spring day, Sir.

Adm. H.: Yes, it's a lovely day, isn't it?

Q: It is indeed. Today I think you plan to talk about your period of service from October 1941 to May 1943 when you served as chief of staff to the Commander-in-Chief, Atlantic Fleet.

Adm. H.: That's right. First of all, Admiral E. J. King, who was then a vice admiral and Commander-in-Chief of the Atlantic Fleet with his flag in the Augusta. The Augusta was based largely on Newport, Rhode Island, in those days. There was a brief sortie up to Casco Bay during the early weeks of my incumbency of the post of chief of staff to Admiral King. That was without any great incident. The first thing of importance that happened and it was not very many weeks after I reported to Admiral King was the attack on the fleet at Pearl Harbor.

Q: Before that, however, this was the period of so-called neutrality and we were maintaining a kind of patrol, were we not? Would you tell me about that?

Adm. H.: Yes, the so-called Neutrality Patrol. There's nothing very much that stands out about that. It was a patrol that was maintained not very far off our coast by destroyers, and it was a patrol of watchfulness because there were incidents in those days of submarine attacks on shipping in North Atlantic lanes. I think it was largely to keep an eye on this that we were maintaining the so-called Neutrality Patrol off our northeast coast particularly and watching the transatlantic shipping lanes.

Q: In case of an attack on one of our merchant ships, we were prepared for offensive action?

Adm. H.: Well, of course, we were prepared to defend shipping, the safeguard of our presence, you might say.

Q: What was Admiral King like as the commanding officer? What was he like to serve with?

Adm. H.: Admiral King at that time was living aboard the flagship. His wife and family were down here in Washington, at the home where they had been for quite a number of years. Admiral King's only recreation that I could recall would be to go ashore in the latish afternoon and take a walk and be back on board at dinner time. We were in Newport all of that period, except the one expedition that I mentioned up to Casco Bay. I think the Casco Bay expedition was really more or less for the purpose of surveying at firsthand the characteristics of Casco Bay as a potential fleet base of sorts.

Q: Did he fully expect the outbreak of hostilities?

Adm. H.: No, I can't say that he did. Of course, the situation was tense, there was no question of that. At that time we were actually, of course, within six weeks of the outbreak of war. The Japanese, as you recall, had representatives in our country, in Washington, and they were talking very earnestly with our administrative command. But I don't think there was a real feeling that war was imminent.

Q: What particular duties were you able to perform for Admiral King as his chief of staff?

Adm. H.: The duty of being his right-hand man as much as possible, keeping an eye on the functioning of the fleet staff. The actual operations of our forces in the Atlantic at that time were, as I recall it, of the simplest because we had to keep an eye on what was going on in the North Atlantic without making ourselves obtrusive.

Q: Was it easy to serve him as his right-hand man?

Adm. H.: I presume that that's the function of a chief of staff.

Q: But he had a reputation of being somewhat difficult as a commanding officer. Did you experience that?

Adm. H.: No, I don't recall that I ever had any difficulty in dealing with him. He was very much in command of the situation himself and knew what was going on. In his dealings with the staff, through me largely, and his dealings with me things were very smooth, as far as I can recall. I myself was staying on board pretty regularly until Admiral King returned aboard from his afternoon walks and things were more or less settled for the day, then I would get permission to go ashore. My wife was living in Newport at that time and I was able to be at home from, say, about five or six in the afternoon until the next morning.

Q: While he kept the shop on board the *Augusta*!

Adm. H.: Yes. Well, of course, there was always a flag duty officer of some seniority to maintain the routine of the ship.

I don't remember any break during that period other than that one visit to Casco Bay.

Q: That was a very brief tour with King, however, wasn't it? It came to an end shortly after your arrival?

Adm. H.: Yes, it was from somewhere around the middle of October, as I recall it, until let's say somewhere around the middle of January when Admiral King was succeeded by Admiral Ingersoll. I don't remember the date of that exactly. It was a few weeks after the Pearl Harbor attack.

Q: How did King act with the news of Pearl Harbor? Were you with him then?

Adm. H.: Yes, I was with him. That, as you remember, was a Sunday morning, but our routine on the flagship was about the same on Sunday as it was any other day. I was on the job that day, just as though it were a weekday. When luncheon was over in the Admiral's mess, he withdrew to his cabin, as he customarily did after luncheon, and I made my way to the little cubby of an office of sorts that I had in the *Augusta*. I had hardly settled down to my desk to have a look at what might come next when the orderly came in and handed me a dispatch, which was the famous dispatch of that Sunday reading, in effect, the Japanese have attacked our fleet at Pearl Harbor, this is not a drill, repeat this is not a drill.

I took that immediately to Admiral King in his cabin and simply handed it to him. He read it without comment. I have been asked at various times what Admiral King's reaction was when he was informed that we were at war with Japan, and I racked my brains to remember what his first words were. His first words were silence!

Q: But when they did come out?

Adm. H.: No, no, I don't remember any subsequently.

Q: What kind of action did you take in the fleet at that point?

Adm. H.: There wasn't any immediate change in the disposition and action that was being taken in the Atlantic Fleet. Of course, the Admiral was summoned to Washington very quickly and was gone for several days and I was taking care of the routine, which didn't change very much immediately as far as the Atlantic Fleet was concerned.

It wasn't very long, of course, before Admiral King was summoned to Washington on a permanent basis, on a wartime basis, and Admiral Ingersoll came to Newport and to the Augusta as his relief.

Q: Did Admiral King discuss with you the kind of job he was taking over?

Adm. H.: I don't suppose that Admiral King knew right away what dispositions were going to be made by Washington, and I don't recall myself just how long he was in Washington when he first went down there. I think he was made CinCUS in a matter of a very few weeks, according to my recollection, and Admiral Ingersoll took over his duties as C-inC, Atlantic, virtually at the time that Admiral King went to Washington on a permanent basis.

The administration of the Atlantic Fleet had no great degree of switch from our standby basis of watchfulness before the war to the routine that was carried on after the war came on. Of course, it did mean right away a greater degree of surveillance and supervision, the organizing and protection of convoys, and all that sort of thing because it began more or less immediately, but the transition in the Atlantic Fleet was not one that required a great deal of change in our modus of operation. It was a matter of volume. The escort of convoys became the big activity almost immediately and that grew as the war went on, and the number of forces that we could assign to it continued to grow. But there was a very quick transition from our status of watchfulness to our status of actually guiding and protecting the shipping.

Q: It was almost a change in name only, wasn't it?

Adm. H.: In a way it was because it required larger forces and greater subdivision of operations when we went to the actual protection of convoys.

Q: What sort of know-how did we have for that situation? We hadn't been in a war situation for many years and all of a sudden here we were with the obligation of organizing convoys and escorting them. How did you go about this?

Adm. H.: The organizing of the convoys was largely in the hands of the district commanders. The escorts were provided by the fleet, as was a certain amount of local escort by the local forces. Our principal job was the organizing of the escort forces and the distribution and administration of those forces in cooperations with the district commanders. Of course, later with the cooperation also of British and Canadian elements who were already in the business of protecting convoys.

Q: How many escort vessels did you think it necessary to assign to a given convoy?

Adm. H.: That would depend upon the size of the convoy. Normally, I think we were able to assign approximately a division of destroyers to the principal convoys. As I say, the Canadians were able to supply escorts. The Allies over in Europe were handling the same thing at the other end. There were Norwegian forces that were concerned too.

Q: Our responsibility was to escort a convoy to a mid-ocean point, was it not?

Adm. H.: By and large.

Q: And then turn it over to the British?

This must have entailed some rather close liaison with the British and the Canadians, did it not?

Adm. H.: Well, as far as the administration of the Commander-in-Chief, Atlantic, was concerned, our liaison was not close. That was largely a matter for the local authorities, the district commanders, and I think Washington perhaps had more to do with that than we did.

Q: Did Admiral Ingersoll approach his job in a manner somewhat different from Admiral King when he came on board?

Adm. H.: As far as the administration of the Fleet was concerned, I wouldn't say that there was a marked transition.

Q: He continued to use the Augusta as his flagship?

Adm. H.: The Augusta didn't remain the flagship for very long. Replacing the Augusta was perhaps a bit of a problem.

Q: Why was it necesary to replace her?

Adm. H.: So as to release the Augusta, because the principal function of an Atlantic Fleet flagship in those days was not to have a mobile fighting base but to have a base which was thoroughly equipped with communications. The initial solution to that situation was by establishing the Atlantic Fleet headquarters virtually ashore, except that it was set up in the old frigate Constellation, which had been berthed alongside the pier at the Naval Training Station, Newport, for a considerable number of years. It was possible to convert the living spaces on the Constellation very quickly to offices and stateroom accommodations for the Commander-in-Chief and his staff, and also to install the necessary telegraph communications et cetera. That's what was done.

Q: Did the Constellation retain her name as the flagship?

Adm. H.: Oh, yes. That was all accomplished in the space of a very few weeks. Of course, it was facilitated by the fact that the flagship Augusta had been based on Newport for a considerable period and the Constellation was available right there alongside the pier, and the installation of the necessary communications and the setting-up of the necessary office spaces and living space for the staff wasn't a tremendous problem.

I know it had been accomplished by some time in January.

Q: That limited your mobility, did it not?

Adm. H.: Yes, and eventually it was recognized that the Commander-in-Chief, Atlantic, needed to have a degree of mobility and the Navy converted a very large private yacht to that purpose, known as the Vixen. I'm not sure whether she had been the Vixen before the Navy took her over. I think not. I think she had a different name, but what it was escapes me at the moment. Of course, the Vixen had to be provided with office spaces and communications in order to be fitted for flagship use. She didn't require any great physical alterations. She required the installation of connections rather than conversion of her spaces.

Q: Once you had her as the flagship, did the Commander-in-Chief make trips?

Adm. H.: Yes. Although in the early part of the war, Newport continued to be the base, the Commander-in-Chief did make some short visits to other areas and eventually, when the planning of joint operations with the Army became a principal activity, the <u>Vixen</u> left Newport and based for a considerable period on Hampton Roads where the joint planning for the invasion of North Africa was carried on. As a matter of fact, that joint planning at Hampton Roads was really carried on mostly at a location ashore, but having the Commander-in-Chief and his staff close aboard the joint planning headquarters of course was a very considerable advantage.

Q: What role did you, as chief of staff, have in this planning effort for North Africa, the Torch Operation?

Adm. H.: I had a very small role in the planning of that invasion. As a matter of fact, I had almost none because the joint planning staff - Army and Navy planning staff - was set up with its headquarters ashore there at Hampton Roads. The business of the staff on the <u>Vixen</u> went forward much as usual without a direct connection with the joint staff that was planning Torch.

Q: But it did involve supplying a great number of additional escort vessels, did it not? They had to be obtained from somewhere.

Adm. H.: For the organization of the invasion, yes, but the detailed plans for Torch were formulated by a separate joint staff based ashore.

Q: What control did Commander-in-Chief, Atlantic, exercise over the units of our fleet that were soon stationed in the British Isles?

Adm. H.: None, as long as they were on station in that area. They then came under Commander, Naval Forces, Europe, which before long was Admiral Stark.

Q: Did you have anything to do with the organization of convoys to Iceland and then from Iceland to Murmansk?

Adm. H.: You mean did I personally?

Q: Or the staff of the Commander-in-Chief?

Adm. H.: Commander-in-Chief, Atlantic?

Q: Yes.

Adm. H.: No, I don't remember that we had any direct duty in connection with the organizing of the forces. We supplied the escorts.

Q: It must have been a very difficult task to supply more and more escorts when we weren't turning them out that rapidly from our shipbuilding yards, were we?

Adm. H.: Well, of course, the expansion was enormous and there were a great many activities concerned with that expansion and the training of forces and supply of forces and so on. The Commander-in-Chief, Atlantic, was by and large the supplier of escorts.

Q: Yes, but he had to get them from somewhere in order to supply them?

Adm. H.: They came largely from the destroyer forces of the Atlantic Fleet, as far as our escort responsibilities went.

Q: You had another large area of responsibility which required destroyers as well, and that was antisubmarine warfare along the Atlantic coast and into the Gulf of Mexico. Tell me about that.

Adm. H.: That was largely the local defenses. I don't recall that we had any organization for which the Atlantic Fleet was responsible in the way of hunter/killer operations. Our responsibility was largely in providing escorts, not carrying out hunter/killer business.

Q: The citation that was given you when you were awarded the Legion of Merit said specifically that your "judicious counsel and clear perception in escort of convoys and anti-submarine operational problems contributed vitally to the successful conduct of the operations."

Adm. H.: The business of escorts for convoys was almost entirely an antisubmarine operation. We were not fearful, you might say, at any time that any German gunboats or cruisers or anything of that sort would be at large, preying on our convoys in the North Atlantic, but we knew that submarines were.

Q: Well, and in that early period it was a very serious menace, was it not, along the coast, especially as it pertained to the tanker traffic?

Adm. H.: Yes, and the way that was countered was by escort of the convoys. There was very little in the way of hunter/killer operations when it came to the antisubmarine effort. The escort of convoys was the principal answer to the submarines.

Q: I know that a concerted effort in this direction was made in the Caribbean Command out of San Juan. How were Admiral Hoover's efforts coordinated with those of Admiral Ingersoll?

Adm. H.: I don't recall that there was any great degree of coordination required with the Caribbean Command. Who was down there at the time, did you say?

Q: Admiral John Hoover..

Certainly some of these tankers coming out of the Gulf of Mexico went through the Caribbean Command and continued into the North Atlantic Command. Therefore, there must have been an overlap of some sort?

Adm. H.: I don't recall that that required any great degree of collaboration, once the system was set up, and I don't remember that the submarine menace, so-called, was ever very great when it came to those areas off to the south, the Caribbean areas. There wasn't much submarine activity there that I can recall.

Q: Oh, yes, there was. At least according to Admiral Hoover, there was a very great deal and it was a matter of tremendous concern to them. We lost so many tankers and we couldn't afford to lose them.

Very shortly, in the war effort in the Atlantic, the Tenth Fleet came into existence in Washington. As you probably recall, it was largely concerned with intelligence, the location of German submarines in the Atlantic and the indication of their location to the fleet commanders. Did this affect your operations?

Adm. H.: I don't recall that it did to any large extent. Our efforts were largely concerned with ensuring safe convoy of ships from our east coast to Europe, where the principal war effort was going on. I don't remember very much about coordination with the Caribbean.

Q: During your time with the North Atlantic Fleet, were the jeep carriers coming into the Atlantic? The small aircraft carriers converted from Liberty ships?

Adm. H.: I don't recall that they were asfar as the anti-submarine effort was concerned.

Q: That's what they were intended for.

Adm. H.: No, I don't remember that up to the time I left the Atlantic Fleet that was a considerable factor. I left in the spring of 1943.

Q: Yes, and that probably was a little early for the jeep carriers.

Adm. H.: I think so, yes.

Q: You said a little earlier that there was no danger of any enemy cruisers or anything of that sort. The Germans did have converted passenger ships armed as cruisers operating in the South Atlantic. Did they ever touch on your own territory?

Adm. H.: No, not that I can recall.

Q: Remember, they were called XCLs, raiders, they were?

Adm. H: In Admiral Ingram's command?

Q: During the time you were there, the large Cunard liners, the Queen Mary and the Queen Elizabeth, were trafficking across the North Atlantic carrying troops. Was this a matter of particular concern to you people?

Adm. H.: I don't remember that it was as distinguished from other convoys. It doesn't register with me, particularly.

Q: They went largely unescorted, of course.

Adm. H.: Relying on their speed, and evasion.

Q: Yes.

I do believe that during that time Prime Minister Churchill came over once or twice to North America, did he not, and this must have been something that was called to your attention?

Adm. H.: I don't remember that we were ever alerted in Headquarters, Atlantic Fleet, to a Churchill visit, as distinguished from other escorted shipping.

Q: We made a very particular effort to send over as many fighter planes as we could and, of course, they were not long-legged and they had to be transported in various ways.

Adm. H.: No, I don't remember that traffic as distinguished from other escorted traffic.

Q: Do you remember any specific events that concerned Admiral

Ingersoll as a man? About the time when Ingersoll was there and how thoughtful he was of you and your comfort, even though it was wartime. Tell me about that.

Adm. H.: Well, of course, our time in the Constellation differed a good bit from the time in the Vixen because the purpose of acquiring the Vixen and putting her into service as a somewhat mobile flagship was based on the necessity for the Commander-in-Chief, Atlantic, to move about a bit. In the Constellation we were absolutely dependent upon being right there alongside the pier in Newport because that's where the offices were, that's where the communications were, and that's where the staff was. So the acquiring of the Vixen made a great deal of difference in the style of the Commander-in-Chief, Atlantic, because he was able to move around. He wasn't confined to Newport any longer, and he did move around, more particularly during the time the Torch operation was being planned, the invasion of North Africa. He was in the Vixen at Hampton Roads, as I said a while ago. He was no longer in Newport. But even though we were in Newport we had our staff and our records and everything else the Commander-in-Chief needed to carry on his business.

Q: I was referring particularly to what Mrs. Hustvedt told us off tape, that when Admiral Ingersoll came to the command he was very considerate of you and told you to entertain your friends from Newport on board the Constellation and that sort of thing.

Adm. H.: That was actually minimal. I think we had one dinner aboard the Constellation.

Q: But it does indicate the fact that, even though it was wartime, you did have a bit of social life. It wasn't all just war.

Adm. H.: That's true, and I guess it's particularly true of the time when the war had settled down to what you might call a routine, if a war can be routine. There was a time when the activity of the Atlantic Fleet was certainly centered upon the escort of convoys and, once that was organized and in operation, it had settled down not to a routine because there were always unexpected things, but at least to a fairly well organized activity.

Q: What I was trying to draw out from you - I mean, I remember the old adage about "all work and no play" you know and what it does to someone, I'm glad to know that this wasn't completely necessary, all work, in time of war as well, that the Navy recognized the need for relaxation and pleasure and what have you. So I was trying to round out the narrative and add this aspect of your tour of duty.

Adm. H.: Well, I don't know how I can expand on what we've already had to say about that.

On the personal side, I had been selected for promotion

in the summer of 1941 and my number came up just about the time we got into the war. I was actually in receipt of my commission early in February of 1942 and it so happened that a week or two later Admiral Ingersoll was called to Washington for conference and expected to be gone for a couple of days. Before he left he said to me, "When I take off for Washington tomorrow, I want you to break your flag." So, very dutifully, when Admiral Ingersoll left the ship the next morning, my two-star flag went up on the Constellation, replacing his three-star flag. That was the first time my flag was ever shown.

Q: I'm glad you recalled that from the photograph.

Adm. H.: I thought of it as soon as I saw those pictures.

Q: I note on the engagement calendar for that period that you frequently engaged in bowling?

Adm. H.: In Newport?

Q: Yes.

Adm. H.: I suppose that was a once-a-week feature, as near as I can remember. Isn't that correct?

Mrs. H.: That's right.

Adm. H.: Well, as the war went on, of course, it settled into something of a routine at times and we did have some opportunities for recreation of one kind or another, including a weekly session at bowling. That was a small group of, I suppose, a dozen or so people.

Q: This included the wives?

Adm. H.: Yes, it included wives.

Q: Tell me about your living quarters there in Newport. You merely referred to the fact that you had a home there, but you didn't tell me what it was.

Adm. H.: During the time that I was at the War College in 1940-1941, we rented a furnished house on Greenough Place which we found very convenient and very suitable. Later on, after I had gone to sea in the North Carolina my wife came on to Brooklyn and our headquarters was at the Towers Hotel, which was on the heights in Brooklyn, fairly convenient to the Navy yard. So when I, some six months later, was ordered to be chief of staff to the Commander-in-Chief, Atlantic, and went back to Newport, we rented a different house, this one on Hunter Avenue, just a few blocks from the house that we had previously occupied on Greenough Place. That was a convenient location, too, of course, and a house of convenient size.

Our daughter and two small boys came on there and lived with grandmother for a matter of quite a few months, as I recall it, during a good part of which time I was away. We had moved to the Vixen in the meantime, and the Vixen, as I have said, was a mobile flagship within her limits and from the time the flag was shifted to the Vixen the Commander-in-Chief was very largely separated from Newport. We were at Philadephia at one time for a matter of weeks.

Q: What would have taken you to Philadelphia?

Adm. H.: I don't remember that there was any special reason for going to Philadelphia, except that there was a berth available there at the naval base and I presume that reasonable proximity to Washington was one of the factors. We were there, I think, not longer than three weeks to a month, something of that kind. I've already mentioned that when the planning for the Torch operation, the invasion of North Africa, became active we shifted down to Hampton Roads.

Q: When you went on trips like that in the Vixen, what kind of escort did you have for her?

Adm. H.: I can't answer that very fully because I don't remember myself just what the escort arrangements were. I would presume that we didn't go to sea between Newport and Hampton Roads, for instance, without something in the way of an escort, but I can't recall what it was.

During the period when the Commander-in-Chief in the Vixen was based on Hampton Roads when the planning for the

Torch invasion of North Africa was active, we had several visitors of considerable interest. These visits were almost daily and included General Patton, who always came aboard wearing his fighting uniform, so to speak, packing two ivory-handled guns on his hips -

Q: That was his trademark!

Adm. H.: Yes - and we were also visited several times by Samuel Eliot Morison, who was gathering material for his naval histories. Admiral Hewitt, who was to command the invasion, of course, was a frequent visitor on board the <u>Vixen</u> because he was participating actively in the planning that was going on at the time.

Q: Well, Sir, in May of 1943 you left the North Atlantic command to take command of battleships in the Atlantic. Tell me about the scope of that operation.

Adm. H.: I was detached from the staff of the Commander-in-Chief, Atlantic, and was made Commander, Battleships, Atlantic, which actually was a type command job which didn't mean that I had an assembled force of ships under my command, as such, but I commanded that type insofar as it was then present in the Atlantic.

Q: How many of our battleships were in the Atlantic?

Adm. H.: Broadly speaking, there were those that were going

into commission at that time and going through shake-down et cetera, plus the Alabama, South Dakota - Alabama being newly commissioned, South Dakota having undergone repair of battle damage which she received in the Pacific, and at the time that I went to that command, I think it was primarily to take command of a division which consisted of the South Dakota and Alabama, and to join with the British Home Fleet based on Scapa Flow.

My operating command, as distinguished from the type command, consisted of those two battleships plus, I think, a destroyer division as escort - a division of five ships which I can't name offhand. And we proceeded in April of that year to Scapa Flow, in the Orkneys, and joined up with the British Home Fleet operating out of that base under the command of Admiral Sir Bruce Fraser, Royal Navy.

Q: What was our purpose in having battleships with the Home Fleet?

Adm. H.: I think the purpose at that time was largely connected with the fact that the German Tirpitz and Scharnhorst were in commission and active and, at least during a part of that year, were holed up in north Norway. I think that it was as a counter to the Tirpitz and Scharnhorst, and also perhaps as a backup connected with the Mediterranean operations that followed the invasion of North Africa.

That stay with the Home Fleet lasted from April to somewhere around the 1st of August, as I remember, and was a very interesting experience for me and, I presume, for the rest of the personnel under my command. We carried on a certain degree of maneuver exercises with the ships of the Home Fleet and had some target practice.

One of the interesting events was receiving a visit from the First Lord of the Admiralty and Admiral Stark, who was our Commander, Naval Forces, Europe. They came up together and I was privileged to be host to Mr. Alexander, the First Lord, in view of the fact that I had a sea cabin in the South Dakota, which I occupied when we were at sea anyhow. I was able to turn over my regular cabin to the First Lord and make him quite comfortable, I think. During the time that they were with us, the South Dakota and Alabama did some firing of antiaircraft guns against a sleeve target towed by one of our own planes. That was of interest to both of them, I think. I don't believe at that time Admiral Stark had had an opportunity to see an antiaircraft practice by one of the new battleships of our fleet that had a rather awesome battery of antiaircraft guns, including those defined as double-purpose guns in the gun houses plus the antiaircraft machine guns that had been installed during the war. I think that was an event that interested both of them very much.

Q: The Royal Navy had enough force to take care of either the Tirpitz or the Scharnhorst, didn't they?

Adm. H.: Yes, I would say so. As a matter of fact, the ships that the British had at Scapa Flow at that time were rather on the formidable side. They had, at the time we were there, never less than two modern battleships, including the flagship Duke of York and the King George V, plus cruisers and destroyers. But I would suppose that we were also a sort of ready reserve in case the operations in the Mediterranean required further support.

Q: Did you get involved in any of the operations to Murmansk, the convoy operations?

Adm. H.: No, not directly. I don't remember that we were called upon for any direct support of convoys at the time I was there at Scapa with the battleships.

Q: And you didn't leave Scapa and go down to the Mediterranean at all, did you?

Adm. H.: No. The only movement that we made during that period at Scapa was local, for exercises, including some gunnery exercises.

Q: Would you distinguish between the two different task groups that you commanded in that year?

Adm. H.: The first one was the battleship pair, which I have just mentioned, together with a beefed-up division of destroyers as escort. We were re-called with almost no notice early in August, which I'm sure was due to the fact that the fleet in the Pacific could stand reinforcement, and when the South Dakota and Alabama were returned to the East Coast it wasn't long before they were on their way to join the forces in the Pacific.

Incidentally, that re-call brought about a bit of personal disappointment to me in that the King was scheduled to make a visit to the fleet at Scapa and, in connection with his visit, I was to be his host at a luncheon on board the South Dakota. The re-call came about a week before that event was scheduled.

Q: After returning to the States you went back to Scapa Flow with a second task force?

Adm. H.: Yes.

Q: That consisted of what?

Adm. H.: When the South Dakota and Alabama group returned to our East Coast, the two battleships were put in motion for the Pacific and I transferred my flag to the Iowa, which had been undergoing its shake-down during the summer. I then had my flag in the Iowa for the remaining months of the summer and of the early autumn.

The Iowa and her sister New Jersey had been commissioned during the early part of that year and had completed their shake-downs and were brought together and organized as Battleship

Division 7 under my command. We operated together in the New England area for a short time and at the end of that exercise period we wound up at Argentia, in Newfoundland, for a short period of exercise based on that area.

Incidentally, one of the interesting incidents connected with that little stay based on Argentia was the fact that there was present in Newfoundland at that time a commission of the British Parliament which was studying, I believe, the relationship of the Maritime Provinces to the rest of the empire and, I think, was expected to make recommendations regarding some changes in the administration of those provinces. My classmate, Jesse Oldendorf, was in command of a shore base at Argentia at the time and he asked me whether I would like to invite the commission to have lunch with me on the *Iowa*. He thought that they might be interested in the ship, she being one of the very latest that we had to offer at the time.

I was glad to do it and, accordingly, had the commission on board to a luncheon together with Oldendorf and my two commanding officers of battleships and one or two others - I've forgotten who. That was a very pleasant occasion and I think the MPs were interested in seeing something of the ship, and it probably gave them a little welcome break in their study of affairs in Newfoundland and Labrador, as well as Prince Edward Island. The gentlemen themselves were very interesting as a group, as one would expect. One of them was a British humorist, whose name is practically a household word in this country as well as in Britain, A. P. Herbert.

Q: He was on board?

Adm. H.: Yes, he was one of the group. I have a picture taken on that occasion.

Another interesting encounter connected with that stay in Argentia. I was invited by Admiral Oldendorf to be his guest at a dinner at his headquarters ashore, and he had perhaps half a dozen of the senior members of his staff messing with him, including a lieutenant commander, I think he was at the time, in the Naval Reserve who a few years after that became the governor of Massachusetts.

I was able to take my division with the destroyer escort out for one exercise, off Argentia, and either that evening or the following evening I received a dispatch ordering me to proceed to Britain as relief of Admiral Bernhard my classmate Alva Bernhard who had been operating out of Scapa with the British Home Fleet with a command which consisted of the aircraft carrier Ranger, the heavy cruisers Augusta and Tuscaloosa, plus a division of destroyers. I packed up overnight and the next morning I was on board a plane which Admiral Oldendorf had supplied me from his command to fly up to the air station at Gander Lake, which was, of course, the principal way station on the air route to Europe.

Q: A rather bleak place, too, wasn't it?

Adm. H.: Yes. Well, it was an hour or so, I suppose. I got up to Gander just about lunch time and I think it was before I had left the luncheon area that I was intercepted by an aide from the office of the commanding officer who informed me that Secretary Knox was expected to touch down early that afternoon on his way to Europe. Well, it was incumbent on me to pay my respects to the Secretary when he arrived, so I was there waiting when the plane came in and when he disembarked I stepped forward and rendered my best salute and said, "Good morning, Mr. Secretary." It so happened that he remembered me, he recognized me, undoubtedly because of the fact that a couple of years before he had been present when the North Carolina was commissioned. He said, "What are you doing here?"

I said, "I'm on my way to Britain to relieve Admiral Bernard, who's going out to the Pacific," and he said, "Why don't you come with us?" I said, "Mr. Secretary, I'd be delighted." Well, the upshot was that the Secretary was traveling on a quite commodious plane.

Q: Much more comfortable than the one you were on!

Adm. H.: Yes, I think so! He had two staff officers with him, and the plane, as it so happened, had a little sort of emergency cabin that was midway between the pilot's space and the space farther aft that contained seats for perhaps a dozen passengers and storage space for a certain amount of baggage. Well, I found that I was expected to share accommodations with the Secretary, so when we turned in not long after that, out over the Atlantic, I got up in the upper berth and the Secretary was in the lower berth and that's the way we went across.

We arrived at Prestwick the following morning, not long after we'd had our breakfast on the plane, and we were met there by a special train that had come up from London to take the Secretary and his party down to London. Admiral Stark had come up on the train. To make a long story short, I was then able to thank the Secretary for the lift and go about my own business, and I was soon in touch with a young liaison officer there who incidentally had been on board the South Dakota when I was at Scapa Flow with the Home Fleet a few months previous. He was the son of Samuel Eliot Morison, and inside of an hour or so there was a light plane of sorts that was available for me to board with my hand baggage, and we flew from Prestwick to Rosyth, where we made a stop, and then headed for Scapa. That was a brilliant afternoon in the early fall, in October, if I remember correctly. There was a bright sun and there had been a lot of recent rain and all Scotland was dripping like a sponge. We were crossing over little lochs and tarns and dripping mountainsides all the way from Edinburgh up to the Orkneys. That was quite a remarkable flight on that account. I have a very vivid recollection of it.

Q: A vivid picture you paint.

Adm. H.: It was a picture all the way.

I was met at Kirkwall, in the Orkneys, by a boat from the fleet. I don't remember whether it was one of our boats or a British boat. Anyhow, it was not long before I was on board the ship at Scapa, the ship being the <u>Ranger</u>, which had been Admiral Bernard's flagship for some time and was to be my flagship then for the rest of the autumn.

I fell heir to Admiral Bernhard's staff He left all of his staff behind him, so that I was in the unusual situation of a non-flyer commanding a group that was founded on a flyer. I had a good staff, and the chief of staff was an old friend whom I had helped to bring up on board the <u>Burns</u> in the early twenties when he went to the <u>Burns</u> almost straight out of the Naval Academy, Fred Boone. You probably know Fred Boone, don't you?

Q: Oh, yes.

Adm. H.: He lives not far from here.

There I was back with the Home Fleet, but with an entirely different outfit.

Q: Did it have a different mission from the one you had earlier in the year?

Adm. H.: It was certainly equipped for different duty, but as far as the mission was concerned it was pretty much as the other one had been, support of the British forces.

It wasn't long before Secretary Knox's visit to Britain was capped by a visit to the fleet. Admiral Stark came up with him. That visit didn't last very long and I don't recall any special incident connected with it. It was not long after that when we had an operation with the Home Fleet which consisted of an attack on the shipping that was passing up and down through the leads on the coast of Norway, in the vicinity of Bodö. Bodö is almost on the Arctic Circle. The air group of the <u>Ranger</u> was the spearhead for that attack, and we had on board in connection with it two or three young Norwegian officers. I am not sure whether they were Norwegian air officers or Norwegian naval officers. I think they were naval officers who were with us for the purpose of taking part in that attack and for the purpose of indicating to our flight groups which of the vessels they might encounter there in the leads were proper subjects for attack and which weren't. That was their function.

Q: Were some of the ships carrying particular cargo that we wanted to sink?

Adm. H.: I don't know whether they were definite cargoes, such as definitely munitions, you mean, and that sort of thing? I never learned whether that was the case or whether it was simply a case of attacking ships that were rather obviously bound for supply of the Germans who were holed up farther north, the Bismarck and Scharnhorst.

I think the Norwegian lads were supposed to know which ships were presumably carrying cargo to the Germans up there. Anyhow, that was the set-up and their function was to go with our air groups and designate targets or non-targets.

Well, the upshot was that our air groups sank or disabled about 17,000 tons of presumable enemy cargo, or ships carrying enemy cargo.

Q: A fairly successful operation, then it was?

Adm. H.: Yes, it was on the whole very successful. We had, I think, two planes shot down by antiaircraft fire, and I never have learned whether the personnel was actually lost or not. I don't know to this day, but I think we lost two planes.

Not long after that the Ranger was sent to Rosyth for repairs, mostly to some plates on her bow structure which had received some damage from ice in the Denmark Strait. While we were there at Rosyth I was directed to go down to London to Admiral Stark's headquarters for consultation down there and for a sort of liaison meeting with opposite numbers - members of my staff and members of Admiral Stark's staff in London.

At the headquarters in London I almost immediately ran into my old friend Paul Bastedo, who had been one of my classmates at the War College, among other things, and Paul invited me to stay with him for the weekend rather than go to a hotel, which the rest of the party did. We got there on a Friday, as I remember it, and on Saturday I was busy at Admiral Stark's headquarters. On Sunday Paul Bastedo and I got into his car and we headed for an expedition out to Windsor. On the way back from Windsor we stopped at the other palace that's in that neighborhood, one of the well-known old royal palaces –

Q: Hampton Court?

Adm. H.: Hampton Court is right. That was a very agreeable break. I don't remember anything else in particular about that visit to London.

We went down on a Friday, as I remember it, and we were there Saturday and Sunday, came back north on the train on Monday.

While the Ranger was there at the dockyard in Rosyth, I received not long after our arrival – I've forgotten whether it was the day after, anyhow, very soon, a very beautiful bouquet of flowers, including roses, which came from Broome Hall with a note from Lady Elgin. She invited me and such of my staff as I cared to bring with me to come to Broome Hall to have tea with her a day or so later, which we accordingly did. I think one of the reasons perhaps why Lady Elgin had issued this invitation was because her young son whose name, I think, was David a youngster of about twelve or so at the time, was very much interested in ships and he had seen the Ranger come into the Firth, a few miles down from Broome Hall, and had identified her from Jane's Fighting Ships or some such source, and he knew that that was the USS Ranger. Anyhow, Lady Elgin invited me to come to tea and bring any of my staff that I wished. So, I accepted and a day or so later I took, I think, three members of my staff, including Fred Boone and a couple of others, and we went up to Broome Hall and had tea with Lady Elgin.

The Earl at that time was in London. Parliament was in session and he was a member of the House of Lords. There was none of her family at home, excepting young David, if that was his name. She had an older son, I think up around eighteen or nineteen, and also a daughter of somewhere around twenty, both of whom were serving in the defenses of Edinburgh, stationed with an antiair battery somewhere or other. Young David during the course of the tea whispered briefly to his mother in a rather embarrassed sort of way, and she said, "Yes, David, if you wish." So young David disappeared. Presently he came back in holding a great big two-handed broadsword. That was the sword of Robert the Bruce. Robert the Bruce, of course, is one of David's ancestors. That was quite an event.

Well, to make a long story short about that, before we left Rosyth, I had Lord Elgin and his lady and the Admiral commanding the dockyard and his lady on board the Ranger for dinner as my guests. Incidentally, in the Ranger I had a flag mess, which I inherited from Alva Bernhard I had not established a flag mess previously on the South Dakota, nor did I later in the Iowa, but Alva Bernard had had a flag mess for senior members of his staff, lieutenant commanders and up, I think it was, messing with him and I carried that forward during the time I was there.

Q: I trust that David got on board the Ranger?

Adm. H.: Yes, it was arranged at that first tea that Lady Elgin and David and I think a governess of sorts were to visit the Ranger on x afternoon, two or three days later. So that was carried out very successfully. I think I mentioned that I had the dinner on the Ranger not long after, and shortly before we left Rosyth I and these same staff officers of mine were invited to have luncheon at Broome Hall. Lord Elgin by that time had come back from London and we had a nice luncheon there. I had wondered a little bit about what I could leave with them in the way of a gift of sorts, and I happened to learn that they were both very fond of shooting, both game in season and target shooting, and that they had been forced to drop it because of the fact that ammunition wasn't available. So I found that I could get a few boxes of shot gun shells that would fit their fowling pieces, and I took shot gun shells up to give them as a parting gift.

That was an interesting stay there. I got over to Edinburgh

for a very short sightseeing expedition, plus acquiring a present for my own lady. I brought her a bolt of Scottish plaid, which she had made into a very good-looking suit later on.

Q: That was a very valuable present!

Adm. H.: It was good-looking, wasn't it?

Mrs. H.: Rather. I still have it.

Adm. H.: Not long after that we were elected to take part in the replenishment of the garrison, technical personnel and facilities of a Norwegian radio station in Spitzbergen, which had been dispersed by a landing party from a German submarine. The Tuscaloosa of my command took aboard the Norwegian replacements with their gear et cetera - let me see now, there was the Ranger, the Tuscaloosa, the Augusta, and my regular destroyer escort, and the British battleship Anson, which carried the flag of Admiral Sir Henry Moore. We were up in the Spitzbergen area, which I think is in the latitude of somewhere between 78 and 80 North, during fairly late October and it was a bit chilly. We wore our winter clothes mostly on the topside in those days.

That relief expedition was carried off without incident.

Q: Why such a formidable task force for this operation? Were you afraid the Tirpitz would come out?

Adm. H.: There was that possibility, of course, but it wasn't formidable except for the fact that there was an able aircraft carrier and one battleship, Sir Harry's. Of course, if the Germans in any way had learned of that expedition they might have looked upon that as a neat little set-up - an American carrier and a couple of cruisers - unless there was a big fellow along.

Anyhow, that was quite an interesting expedition. That was my all-time farthest north and that, as I recall it, was to within about 900 miles of the pole, about as far as from here to Chicago.

WE were recalled somewhere along in early November, as I remember it, and thereby missed by a matter of weeks being in the encounter with the Germans up around North Cape. That battle around North Cape with the Germans, I think, was on Boxing Day - isn't that early in December?

Q: Boxing Day is the day after Christmas.

Adm. H.: Oh, is it? Well, it seems to me that that encounter between the Germans and the Home Fleet was on Boxing Day. We'd been gone for about a month then.

It was not long after the expedition to Spitzbergen that we were recalled, and when we got back to this side I returned to the _Iowa_ and picked up my battleship staff there and prepared to go about my business. In the meantime, the _Iowa_ had been off on her own, taking the President to Casablanca and FDR had been occupying my cabin in my absense! But it wasn't long before we were slated to pick up the New Jersey which had gone into commission in the meantime - she had been operating with us but that had amounted to a shakedown cruise, I think for the New Jersey. So it was time for me to go back and pick up my regular command and go back to the Iowa. She was ordered to the Pacific early in January.

Interview No. 9 with Vice Admiral Olaf M. Hustvedt, U.S. Navy
(Retired)

Place: His residence in Washington, D.C.

Date: Tuesday afternoon, 30 April 1974

Subject: Biography

By: John T. Mason, Jr.

Q: Admiral, on this perfectly beautiful spring day we're about to resume your story with Chapter 9. You had returned from duty with your battleship at Scapa Flow with the British Home Fleet to the States and picked up your flagship, which had had other duties in the meantime, the battleship Iowa. You were about to be detailed to the Pacific. Do you want to resume your story at that point, Sir?

Adm. H.: That was early in January, as I remember it. You don't have any dates here, do you, for me to pick up?

Q: Yes, of 1944.

Adm. H.: It's my recollection that we left the East Coast on the 5th of January 1944. This was the Iowa and the New Jersey, which was the regular composition of the Battleship Division 7, as then organized. We had a division of destroyers as escort, and we had a destination but I can't remember whether it was given in advance of our leaving the East Coast or not, but it turned out to be Funafuti in the Ellice Islands, and the passage from the East Coast to Funafuti was broken only by transit and refueling at the Panama Canal.

Q: Were there any submarines sighted, or anything of the sort, while you were still in the Atlantic?

Adm. H.: No, there were no incidents that I can recall of any kind whatever in the Atlantic or after making our passage through the Canal. It has occurred to me to wonder whether we may not have made something of a record in speed of transit for a battleship group. I've never tried to check up on it and I couldn't tell you as of now how many miles it is from Boston to Funifuti or Boston to Colon and from there on to Funafuti, but, as I recall it, we never made anything less than 18 knots during that whole cruise.

Q: Well, your battleships came to be known as the fast battleships, did they not?

Adm. H.: They were fast compared to their predecessors, yes. There's no question of that. They were faster as well as larger and more heavily armed. I have heard them called the fast battleships, yes. I have not checked up, as I say, on the figures for that cruise in mileage and time, but suffice it to say, perhaps, that it was a fast transit for heavy ships.

Q: Going through the Canal, was this at all difficult with such huge men-of-war?

Adm. H.: No, I don't remember that there was any more difficulty in servicing those ships than there had been with other ships in which I had transited the Canal. Of course, the Iowa and New Jersey were, you might say, a close fit for the Panama Canal locks, but I don't remember any difficulty whatever. We lingered on the Pacific side just long enough to refuel and perhaps to top off in the way of provisions, I don't remember that.

Q: What sort of process was it to refuel battleships? How long a process?

Adm. H.: Well, of course, that would vary by the degree to which the tanks were empty, but usually it's only a matter of, say, four or five hours. I don't recall any refueling of a battleship that took more than four or five hours. Of course, the old coaling used to be pretty regularly an all-day operation.

I don't recall that we encountered any other shipping or any other traffic of any kind between the Canal and the Funafuti area. We arrived in Funafuti, as I remember it, in the early forenoon and had been picked up not long after daylight by planes from Funafuti which came out presumably to scout for us because they picked us up quite soon after daylight and, as I remember it, more or less escorted us the few hours that were left before we got to our anchorage at Funafuti.

Q: Was that a protected anchorage?

Adm. H.: It's an atoll anchorage, fairly well enclosed and commodious. We joined there the force that was about to move into the Marshall Islands, which was largely a carrier operation, since that particular movement was carried out under the command of Rear Admiral F. C. Sherman, who had his flag in the carrier Bunker Hill.

Our part of the operation connected with the occupation of the Marshalls was, one might say, uneventful. I don't recall that the battleships in that force had much of anything to do prior to the actual occupation of the Majuro atoll, which was our first base.

Q: Only two battleships participated?

Adm. H.: No. As I recall it, that was the beginning of the assembly of what became known as Fast Carrier Task Force that operated more or less as a unit for a number of months after that time. I'm not sure whether we were all assembled at Funafuti or whether some units possibly joined at about the time the base at Majuro was set up.

Q: You didn't actually engage in shore bombardment then?

Adm. H.: Not then, but my division did engage in a shore bombardment within a matter of a few weeks after that against the atoll of Mili. We were joined for that operation by the new carrier Yorktown, as I remember. That operation against Mili was carried out rather early in February, according to my recollection - no, it was March 17th. That was carried out in our operations from Majuro as a base. I would have to go back because I'm getting ahead of myself there.

Q: Yes, tell me about the actual operations at Majuro, what role you played in them?

Adm. H.: The occupation of Majuro, as far as I can remember it, was quite a peaceful occupation. There was no resistance in Majuro or in the immediate vicinity of Majuro. We simply moved in and took possession of the natural anchorage, for which defenses were very quickly set up. I don't remember any real resistance at Majuro or in the immediate vicinity of Majuro.

Q: Did you have a contingent of Marines on board the Iowa?

Adm. H.: We had our regular complement of Marines, but nothing in the way of any part of the Marine expedition. We carried no expeditionary Marines.

Q: Somewhere along in there you bombarded Truk, did you not?

Adm. H.: Yes, that is by air. There was no gun bombardment

of Truk. At least, none that I participated in or that I saw or that I can recall.

During that stay in Majuro there was an organized attack on Truk which I think was largely by air. In the course of that operation the surface ships and cruisers did make a sortie from Majuro and moved over to the Truk area, which was already under attack by our aircraft and, as we arrived in the vicinity of Truk, some ten or twenty miles to the north of Truk, we came under - I'm speaking now of the battleships formation - attack by at least one Japanese plane and also met a formation of two cruisers and two destroyers coming out from Truk, evidently with the purpose of escaping, not with the purpose of engaging us in action. But the cruisers came under fire from our battleships and both were sunk. The destroyers escaped to the westward but at least one of them fired torpedoes at our formation, one of which porpoised ahead of the *Iowa* at a distance of a very few hundred yards.

Our formation continued a bit to the westward past Truk and the circled and actually circumscribed Truk without running into any other enemy forces of any kind whatever. That was an operation that lasted from the forenoon well into the next day before we departed for our anchorage at Majuro, but the only enemy forces that we saw were the two cruisers, which were sunk, and the two destroyers, which escaped, and one or two aircraft. One of those aircraft made a low-level approach against the *Iowa* and dropped a bomb with the evident intention of getting a hit on our bridge. Well, the bomb missed the bridge, but it landed close enough aboard on the far side so that when it detonated somewhat underwater it damaged the plumbing in that part of the ship - interior plumbing - on account of the pressure from the bomb detonation.

Q: That was kind of a close call, was it not?

Adm. H.: That was rather a close call.

Q: You were on the bridge, I take it?

Adm. H.: Yes. I was about to say that it didn't take long after that plane was sighted before it was evident that they meant to attack us - of course, we didn't know what kind of an attack - and the best defense that I could think of for myself personally when the plane dived toward our bridge was to go flat on the deck, which I did! That was a fairly close call.

Q: Were there any injured on the Iowa?

Adm. H.: Personnel injuries? No. The only injury was to the plumbing.

Q: Admiral, what was the state of morale in your battleship contingent?

Adm. H.: It was very high throughout the time that I had my flag in the Iowa, which was from then until nearly the end of October. There were no morale problems, certainly none that were brought to my notice.

The operations of the Fast Carrier Attack Forces, called the Fifth Fleet and Seventh Fleet, proceeded from that time almost without interruption until it finally wound up in the Philippines.

Q: Tell me about some of the conferences you must have attended in preparation for some of these operations. Admiral Turner was about, was he not?

Adm. H.: Admiral Kelly Turner was certainly in some of the areas that we were in, but I did not personally see Admiral Turner during the entire time I was in the Pacific in 1944.

The conferences which I attended were conferences that were held by either Admiral Spruance or Admiral Halsey, who alternated in the fleet command in that area and during that time. You may recall that operations under Admiral Halsey were Third Fleet operations and operations under Admiral Spruance were Fifth Fleet. Of course, the Third Fleet and the Fifth Fleet were identical. That's understood by you as well as by other historians.

Q: You were a part of both fleets?

Adm. H.: Yes, my battleship division was a part of both fleets in their regular turn and was also under Admiral Mitscher's command because it operated constantly with the Fast Carrier Attack Squadrons. It was part of the screen, you might say, of the carrier group.

Q: Could you discern any great difference in the command as exercised by these two men, Halsey and Spruance?

Adm. H.: Not really because my actual personal contact with them was minimal. It occurred only on a very few occasions when a conference was called before the beginning of an operation and as far as the personal characteristics of the two admirals, the Fifth Fleet and the Third Fleet, were concerned I don't think that I could say I noticed a difference of personalities in the top command from one operation to another. It would be very difficult for me to have said about a certain operation that that was characteristic of Halsey or that was characteristic of Spruance.

Q: And yet they were radically different as men?

Adm. H.: As personalities, yes.

During the months or weeks in which I was operating under Halsey's command, I myself was not in a position to notice a difference in the command structure of Halsey or the command structure of Spruance. It didn't really register with me as a difference in approach.

Q: What was the primary purpose in having the fast battleships there for these several operations?

Adm. H.: I would say that the primary importance in having the fast battleships there was to have a counter to possible attack by the Japanese fleet. The Japanese fleet was still in being, as you know, and as a matter of fact they were operating sufficiently so that when it came to the Philippine waters there were actually contacts between ours and their, for instance, in the San Bernardino Strait.

Q: Prior to that, with Saipan and Tinian and the Marianas in general, were you actually anticipating an engagement with the Japanese fleet?

Adm. H.: I don't recall any time when we regarded contact with the Japanese fleet as being imminent, but I left the Pacific about the middle of October of 1944 and it was not long after that when the actual contact came about - that was the San Bernardino Strait and Surigao. Those were fought within a very few weeks after my departure.

Q: When you heard that news, you must have regretted having been called back?

Adm. H.: Oh, yes, I sure did, but there was nothing I could do about it.

Q: In addition to the one air attack you told me about, did you encounter other Japanese air attacks on your battleships?

Adm. H.: Yes. There was an air attack against us, a very small one, during operations in the vicinity of Ponape. I recall that in the rather early morning, off Ponape, we were approached by either two or three - I don't remember which - Japanese planes flying in a very tight formation and very low, probably not more than 200 or 300 feet, and they were headed directly for the Iowa and New Jersey. I don't recall what the character of our formation was at that time otherwise, but they were brought under fire by our antiaircraft batteries and the planes were destroyed when they were probably not more than a mile from our formation and headed right for it. I have been inclined to think that that was possibly the first attempt at a kamikaze attack against our ships because they were actually not much higher at the time they were knocked down than our masthead - maybe a bit more, a few hundred feet - but they were brought under intense fire by our antiaircraft batteries from 5-inch down and both of them were wiped out.

At that time, I believe, the technique of kamikaze attack was not known, not publicized, and I don't think that the time of this incident that we were calling it "kamikaze" because, as I say, kamikaze was new.

Q: It hadn't yet been recognized as a suicide attempt?

Adm. H.: Well, this plane that attacked us off Truk that I've mentioned and dropped a bomb that landed just off the side of the Iowa, that was a very-low-level attack but it was not a kamikaze attack because he didn't crash his plane into the ship. He made a dive and passed overhead probably not more than

200 or 300 feet and that was it. But the two planes that were headed for us off Ponape certainly looked as though they were prepared to crash.

Q: When they came in so low, was your radar able to pick them up readily?

Adm. H.: I doubt whether radar figured in that because this was broad daylight and we saw them coming from several miles away. Of course, we knew that we were near Japanese installations at Ponape. I presume that those particular planes were based on Ponape.

As I recall it we, that is, speaking of the Iowa, fired a few rounds at what appeared to us to be Japanese installations on Ponape without stopping to try to make any finished job. That was just about the time of this sortie which to me appeared to be a typical kamikaze that I read about later on.

Q: And your bombardment, which was brief, was just a passing gesture, was it?

Adm. H.: Practically, yes.

Q: Not a part of any set plan?

Adm. H.: No, not a part of any planned operation.

Q: When did you get into a planned operation of shore bombardment?

Adm. H.: In the Marianas, when the attack was made on Saipan and

Tinian. Battleship Division 7, which was my command, bombarded Tinian in preparation for the landing there.

Q: How much in advance of D-Day did you do this?

Adm. H.: The attack on Saipan and Tinian apparently was in February of 1944, although I don't remember it being quite so early. The shore bombardment, of course, was in preparation for the landing craft to move on in. It was virtually a continuous thing. When the shore bombardment was lifted the boats moved in.

Q: How far were you standing off from the islands?

Adm. H.: I would say, by my recollection, a matter of two or three miles, not much more.

Q: Did the Japanese planes attempt to interfere with your effort in bombardment?

Adm. H.: No. As far as the Tinian sector is concerned there was no Japanese resistance that remains in my mind.

Q: The Tinian amphibious operation was under the command of Admiral Harry Hill. Did you sit in on a conference that he may have held in preparation for it?

Adm. H.: No, there was no pre-landing conference that involved my presence before the Tinian attack. Admiral Lee may have taken part in such a conference. Admiral Lee was in command of the battleships, you know.

Q: The over-all commander?

Adm. H.: In the Fifth Fleet and Third Fleet, Admiral Lee was the over-all commander of battleships. My command was a division. Admiral Lee may have been at a conference prior to the landing. I was not.

What was the date of that operation against the Marianas?

I would like to say something about the operation against Mili atoll.

Q: By all means.

Adm. H.: That was around the 21st of February.

Q: The 17th is the date for Mili.

Adm. H.: About a month later than the activity around Truk.

During the time that we were using Majuro atoll as a base, I was directed to organize and carry out an attack against the atoll of Mili, which lies a few hundred miles southeast of Majuro. Mili was known to be fortified to a certain extent and to be occupied by Japanese ground forces. The operation was to be carried out under my command with my own division, which was the two ships, Iowa and New Jersey, plus the new carrier Lexington -

Q: Under the command of Felix Stump.

Adm. H.: My task was bombardment of Mili atoll by guns and

bombs, I think possibly for the purpose of reducing the capacity of Mili as an armed shore facility and possibly for the purpose of developing the actual Japanese strength at Mili. In any event, my forces consisted of my own division, Iowa and New Jersey, with a destroyer division escort, and a new carrier. The carrier was under the command of Felix Stump, who was possibly recently promoted to flag rank at the time - I don't remember it for sure. At any rate, Stump reported to me prior to the operation and we had a little conference about the making up of the operation order, and I issued an operation order to cover the little task of Mili bombardment.

The day before we were to leave for Mili atoll, before the operation, Admiral Lee informed me that he would like to go along as an observer. He made it quite plain that when he said "observer" he meant "observer," and he actually during the course of the small operation did observe but he did not interpose any orders or indicate that he be looked upon as other than an observer. I had noted in one of the historic publications covering this small operation that it is stated to have been under the command of Vice Admiral Willis A. Lee. That is correct only technically. As I have just stated, Admiral Lee made it perfectly plain to me that he wished to take part purely as an observer and he did so take part. He issued no orders whatever before or during the conduct of the operation.

I presume that the historians have based their accounts on the fact that when Admiral Lee came on board his flag was broken on the Iowa, which was in compliance with the courtesy requirements of the situation, but Admiral Lee did not issue any commands and did not interpose personally in any way whatever during the carrying out of that small operation.

Q: For how long a period were you involved in this operation?

Adm. H.: As I recall it, it was virtually an overnight run from Majuro down to Mili and a bombardment that was carried out during daylight hours involving, as I remember it, one run at suitable range for conducting the bombardment of the main battery, the 16-inch guns, and then a run to closer range to bring the torpedo defense battery into play, and a short bombardment by the torpedo defense battery.

There were no special incidents connected with this bombardment, except that the shore batteries opened up during the second run and made two hits on the Iowa. One of them was not far above the waterline, aft, in the quarter deck area, which did minor damage in an unoccupied storage compartment, and one projectile hit the face plate of turret 2 and, in fragmenting, blew certain small particles in through the sight port and gave a little sprinkling of skin-deep wounds to the turret pointer who was at the telescope just inside.

Q: So he got a Purple Cross!

Adm. H.: He got a Purple Heart for that! I don't think it damaged him very much. It was a minor spray of very minor fragments, which probably had been retarded in going off by ricocheting in the meantime, that came in and hit him in the face.

Q: Usually, what size gun did the Japanese use for their shore emplacements?

Adm. H.: I never learned what the calibers were. I presume that the caliber of the shore batteries there was somewhere in the neighborhood of our 5-inch and 6-inch guns.

Q: Did they have an airfield on Mili?

Adm. H.: I never really learned much about what the character of the Japanese shore installation at Mili was because we moved on from that area very soon after that and didn't return to it. So the actual character of the Japanese installation at Mili was known only vaguely at that time and I've never really learned anything about it since. It couldn't have been very extensive because we saw no indication of a dock structure there. Such guns as they had ashore must have been put ashore in landing craft and couldn't have been of very large caliber.

Q: Actually, you probably could have taken the island in that single operation?

Adm. H.: Yes, if there had been any desire to occupy Mili,

which there wasn't. I think the principal purpose was to develop some knowledge of what there actually was down there at Mili. The capability of Mili couldn't have been very great.

Q: Were similar operations conducted from Majuro on other islands in the area?

Adm. H.: No, that was the only one that I know of, the only one that I ever heard of. Of course, that particular little operation was exploratory, you might say. That filled in the period when we were based in Majuro which might not have been occupied by anything more than drill.

Q: Did they build Majuro into a kind of a fleet base? Did you have supplies at Majuro?

Adm. H.: I can remember being on shore in Majuro not at all. I remember visiting the dentist on board the hospital ship while we were at Majuro, but there were no facilities ashore there for recreation and very rudimentary base facilities of any kind, I'm sure. I don't think the Japanese had any base to amount to anything on Majuro when we moved in there. I can really tell very little about Majuro because we weren't there long and, as I say, I never got ashore there.

Interview No. 10 with Vice Admiral Olaf M. Hustvedt, U.S. Navy
(Retired)

Place: His residence in Washington, D.C.

Date: Tuesday afternoon, 11 June 1974

Subject: Biography

By: John T. Mason, Jr.

Q: All right, Sir, we're going to begin Chapter 10 by having you give us an account of the bombardment of the island of Mili, which was a diversionary operation.

Adm. H.: Within a very few weeks after moving in to the Marshall Islands and establishing the fleet base at Majuro, my division was designated as a part of a group to carry out a gun and air bombardment of Mili Atoll, which is in the chain to the southward of Majuro. In addition to my own battleship division and a destroyer division escort, the aircraft carrier Lexington was designated as the air element of the operation. The Lexington was one of a new class of aircraft carrier which had not been long in the fleet although I believe she had become the flagship of Admiral Mitscher's fast carriers. She was commanded by Captain Felix Stump, who reported to me at Majuro before the operation and who was responsible for the air attack phase of the Mili assault.

Very shortly before the group moved from Majuro to the assault on Mili, Admiral Lee informed me that he would like to accompany the attack group purely as an observer and he, accordingly, came on board the Iowa before we left the Majuro base and naturally remained in the ship until our return to Majuro after the Mili attack had been completed.

I should like to record here my appreciation of the fact that Admiral Lee, although he was a very interested observer of the operation against Mili and spent virtually the entire day and, I am quite certain, the entire period of the air attack and the gun bombardment, on the flag bridge of the Iowa, he never at any time interposed anything which could be interpreted as an interference with the plan which I had issued in my short operation order nor with the movements as they were executed by the forces under my command. His abstention from interposition of any kind with the operation was complete, and I hope that these notes will record my appreciation of the manner in which Admiral Lee carried out his desire to observe the details of the operation.

Q: Now you're going to tell me about the Battle of the Philippine Sea and your battleships' participation?

Adm. H.: Yes. About the 19th of June the Fast Carrier Task Force, to which Battleship Division 7 was regularly attached, came under Japanese air attack, either carrier- or land-based.

That was the beginning of the Battle of the Philippine Sea, so called, insofar as the carrier attack group and its supporting screen was concerned.

On the 20th of June, the following day, the formation was attacked in greater force and a few of the enemy planes penetrated sufficiently far to attack directly the carriers and battleships of the U.S. force. The Iowa and New Jersey, my division, were a part of the battleship screen which had been considerably extended in a defensive formation for the protection of the carriers which were at the center. My flagship, the Iowa, was consequently at a considerable distance from other members of the force so that no close-up view of the various incidents of the attack was afforded. We were able to recognize the fact that South Dakota had been hit, but South Dakota was on the far side of the formation and was, I presume, at least four miles or more from my flagship, the Iowa, and our information with regard to details of damage suffered by various units was derived from later information. Although we could see at times the attacking planes come in and were able to spot what we assumed to be Japanese planes burning on the surface after having been knocked down because of the fact that here and there throughout the area would appear sources of black smoke on the surface which would persist for several minutes, we knew that those smoke sources must represent planes which had been knocked out of the air and which were burning on the surface.

This attack began on the 19th of June with what I think were later identified as land-based Japanese planes and was followed on the 20th by a renewed attack. Admiral Mitscher's force on the 20th was moved to the westward to launch an air attack aimed at the Japanese carriers and other capital ships of the force from which the Japanese air attack had originated, and returning from that attack were overtaken by darkness so the decision was made by Admiral Mitscher to turn on lights to guide his returning planes and to permit their recovery aboard the carrier. That recovery was carried on almost entirely not only after sunset but in the actual dark of the evening.

Battleship Division 7, my command, remained in the Marianas through July, still operating with the Fast Carrier Task Force, carrying on air strikes against Japanese installations which included some on Palau and on Guam. It was during this period, I believe, that my flagship, Iowa, was detached temporarily from the formation to move into the harbor of Garapan Town, in Saipan, to receive from a freighter an important piece of mechanical equipment as a replacement.

The Iowa arrived off Garapan in the early morning and the local commanding general, who had established headquarters in Garapan Town, had a jeep at the landing to take me for a visit to his headquarters. He also suggested that I might want the driver to take a short excursion around the town and near vicinity so that I might observe at firsthand some of the effects of bombardment and to view the terrain over which the assault forces had operated. He also invited me to luncheon with him, which I was glad to accept, and not long after luncheon, the transfer of the equipment to the Iowa being completed, I returned to the ship and we departed to rejoin the task force.

Q: Why did they choose a battleship to carry a piece of machinery?

Adm. H.: No, the piece of machinery was destined for replacement of a similar piece of machinery on board the Iowa, but the machinery had been transported to the area aboard a freighter. It was, of course, only a part of the cargo that that freighter carried as supplies for the operating forces. That was only one item but the practical way to land that piece of equipment on the Iowa for installation in place was to have the Iowa visit the harbor at Saipan and for the freighter to come alongside and transfer it with cranes. It was equipment of such size and weight that taking the freighter alongside as we usually took oilers for refueling was not going to be practical with any certainty, on account of possible sea conditions et cetera. It was a job that was adapted to quiet waters. That was the only reason for the Iowa going in there, to get that important bit of machinery, and I don't remember what it was, whether it was an electric motor of considerable size or just what.

Well, that covers the Battle of the Philippine Sea, after a fashion, and that visit to Saipan I think was very shortly after that. And I think it was probably shortly after that that there occurred a "meeting" with "Red" Ramage on the Parche, which he knew very little about until many months afterwards. Did he ever mention that to you?

Q: No.

Adm. H.: Did I mention it to you?

Q: No. Go ahead and tell it.

Adm. H.: The Fast Carrier Attack Force remained pretty constantly at sea out in that area, except for such times as it would move into one of the atoll bases, such as Majuro, afterward Eniwetok, Kwajalein, Ulithi. Otherwise, we were at sea practically all the time and it was while we were in the Marianas area, somewhere roughly between Guam and Saipan, that Admiral Lee had turned over the operation of the battleships to me for a while and we were temporarily in a separate formation, not in a screen around the carriers. This must have been during - oh, it may have been connected with a fueling period.

At any rate, the position that I was in along toward evening was an independent position, separate from the carrier screen, and with darkness coming on, and we had been informed by dispatch late in the afternoon, as I recall it, that sometime during the evening the Parche would be passing through the area bound eastward. It was actually from one of her patrol areas, off the Japanese coast or in that general sea area between Japan and the Philippines, and she was on her way to Pearl Harbor and was proceeding on the surface with her lights on. Well, we were operating with lights out, so it was presumably incumbent on us to take all necessary steps to identify the Parche when she appeared over the horizon and to keep out of her way, even though we weren't showing any lights. That put the onus on us. I happened to be operating my own unit at that time, so that I had to do the moving of my battleship division, the Iowa and New Jersey, together with our destroyer screen out of the way of the Parche whenever we should identify her light coming over the horizon, which wouldn't be very many miles away.

At the same time, we were not doing very much lingering in one spot either because of the possibility that the Japanese still might have submarines operating in that area. The point of the long story is that I was on the bridge for a considerable time, waiting for a light identifying the Parche to come over the horizon and then making sure that my outfit was moved out of the way. That's what happened. We finally sighted the light almost directly to the west of us and I had to move my outfit southward in the dark several miles to make sure that we wouldn't be in Parche's way, in case he decided to change course a little. And I think Red never knew that we were there, never knew that a formation of battleships had moved out of his way that evening. He may have known, I don't know.

Q: Why was he traveling with his lights on?

Adm. H.: I think because he was going to proceed on the surface and he knew that he was going through an area where U.S. forces, including battleships, carriers, cruisers, destroyers, transports, and what not were operating in considerable numbers and the safe thing for him to do was to proceed on the surface so that they would know where he was. I think that was just a safety precaution. Here, I'm a relatively invisible little fellow with nothing but a conning tower and a few feet of deck showing and I'm going through an area which is just covered with friendly forces that are operating on the surface and, unless they can give me some kind of gangway through their immediate area, I'm going to be up against it. That was the idea. We gave the Parche a free gangway even though she might be changing course a bit for one reason or another. But you can't give her a free gangway unless you can see her. If she's so low-slung that your radar doesn't do much good, it's safer for her to show a light while she's passing through your area.

Well, I've talked about the visit to Saipan and the Parche incident, which I think was probably three or four days after the Battle of the Philippine Sea, and that brings us up to early August.

Q: Now, Sir, do you want to say something about the participation in the Hollandia operations, which came earlier, in March?

Adm. H.: After the operation against Mili atoll, which has been covered in some depth, the next move for the Fast Carrier Group to which the battleships of Admiral Lee's command were attached, towards the end of March we supported air strikes against Palau and Woleai, in the Carolines, and then moved to New Guinea area where the operations in the vicinity of Humboldt Bay were going on, as part of General MacArthur's advance through the East Indies.

Then around the last week of April, we supported by air strikes the Army forces operating at Hollandia and other New Guinea areas, and then wound up with another strike at Truk on the 29th and 30th April. On the 1st of May Battleship Division 7 participated in bombardment of facilities at Ponape in the Carolines, which consisted, I think, of a seaplane base and other facilities. To the best of my recollection, it was while we were passing close to the Ponape base that my Battleship Division came under an apparent kamikaze attack by planes which seemed to be coming directly from the shore base at Pondpe. Either two or three planes in a tight formation, not much more than masthead height, and heading directly toward us. These planes were brought under fire by the antiaircraft guns of both the Iowa and New Jersey, and both, or all three, as the case may be, were splashed some few thousand yards or so from the ships. I could not help wondering later, in reading about the so-called kamikaze attacks by Japanese planes, whether this incident in the Ponape vicinity was the first of the kamikaze attacks because I think we had neither seen nor heard of anything parallel up to that time.

Q: In a sense you were at a loss as to how to deal with them, too, weren't you?

Adm. H.: The only thing we knew to do was to bring them under fire with our antiaircraft batteries, including machine guns, and both Iowa and New Jersey were plentifully supplied with antiair artillery.

That was Ponape. After that operation we returned to Majuro, and that was early in May. The stay at Majuro was from then practically until the operation against the Marianas.

QL Along about that time, late July or early August, you had something happen to one of your eyes?

Adm. H.: Yes. I can't establish a date for that incident and can only estimate it because of the surrounding circumstances. During a period when we had rather frequent alerts against air attack and very likely during late July or early August, I underwent an incident which was to prove somewhat significant in my life, I think, in this way.

After one of the air attack alerts, during which the antiaircraft battery of the *Iowa* was either engaged very briefly or was not actually engaged, the guns of the antiaircraft battery, including the 5-inch twin mounts, had been loaded with live ammunition, and when the incident, whatever it was, had passed I resumed my customary bucket seat which was attacked to the bridge rail on the starboard side of the flag bridge in the *Iowa*. I frequently sat in that bucket seat when I didn't have to be on my feet because during those months in the Pacific when we were at sea I lived on the flag bridge. I didn't live in my cabin. I visited my cabin to take a shower when I could. Outside of that, I didn't occupy my regular cabin at all. I slept on a cot which my Filipino boy rigged for me each evening inside the flag comming tower, which had an entrance on the flag bridge itself. I ate my meals on a dropleaf chart board on the flag bridge. I dropped down to my cabin, which was two flights lower down, when I needed a change of clothing or had an opportunity to take a shower.

After the alert had passed on the occasion of which I'm now speaking, I resumed my bucket seat hung on the bridge rail on the starboard side. The nearest 5-inch twin mount went into securing position, with the guns pointed forward, situated so that it was probably not more than twenty or twenty-five feet abaft my bucket seat on the bridge and probably ten feet lower down the muzzles of the nearest 5-inch gun, I would say it was within twenty-five feet. In relation to the gun, I was forward of it and on the port bow of the gun, about ten feet higher up and about twenty feet farther forward. In other words, my actual separation from the gun breech was probably not more than twenty-five to thirty feet.

Shortly after I sat down, one of the guns of that nearby mount was discharged, with the guns pointing forward, that blast, I would say, was not more than twenty-five to thirty feet from me and I was in the forward cone. It literally blew me out of my chair and I landed on the deck on the bridge, on my feet, and apparently was no worse for the incident, but within a very short period - I don't remember whether it was a matter of hours or whether it was a day - I became conscious of a cloud constantly floating in my vision, in my right eye. The gun muzzle was to my right and below, and it was the right eye that had the cloud in it.

Trying to account for it later, I satisfied myself that what had happened was that the gun blast had actually ruptured something within my eyeball and that the result had been a very small hemorrhage in my eyeball and that this cloud of particles that I was constantly seeing was probably a little cloud of blood, actually. The thing didn't bother me very much. It didn't affect my vision very markedly, except that that little cloud of particles was always there and moving about.

I knew that something had been damaged, even though not seriously. That was later to lead to my visiting the naval dispensary when I got to Washington, matter of probably six weeks to two months afterward, and my consulting the oculist or opthamologist at the naval dispensary in Washington resulted in my being sent to Bethesda for a thorough-going check-up and, to make a long story short, led to my being ordered before a physical retiring board in a matter of weeks.

The retiring board had resulted not from the fact that my eye was injured but from the fact that the physical evidence that was recorded at Bethesda indicated that I had a coronary deficiency. I have lived thirty-odd years since then with the same coronary deficiency, so far as I know, but I had no real reason to put up a strenuous objection to the findings of Bethesda because I had experienced at various times a mild distress after a continuous physical effort. I had been without regular exercise for many, many months. Well, I was before a retiring board by the late autumn of 1945, not very many weeks after I had returned from the fleet.

Q: That must have been 1944?

Adm. H.: 1944, right. That covers the incident of the gun that was unloaded through the muzzle without my being aware of the fact that it was going to take place.

Q: So, they did retire you but they put you to work again?

Adm. H.: I was ordered as a member of the General Board. It was during the month of October that I reported in Washington and went through this examination at Bethesda. It was not until early spring that I had been processed through the retiring board and was actually on the retired list on the 1st of April. That was five or six months later. I don't know just why that retirement process took so long.

Q: What were you doing in the interim here in Washington?

Adm. H.: As soon as I was entered into the retirement process as a result of that examination at Bethesda, I was ordered as a member of the General Board and immediately took up duties as a member of the General Board. I was never hospitalized for anything.

Q: Tell me about your duties on the General Board.

Adm. H.: The General Board, as you know, is a deliberative body that deliberates and reports on questions that are referred to it by the Secretary of the Navy. I don't think it would be appropriate to try to recall here all the matters that were being deliberated on by the General Board during the fifteen or sixteen months that I was a member. I think those are all matters of record.

Q: Yes, but some of them must have been of outstanding interest to you and must have been of some importance to the Navy. Do you recall one or two?

Adm. H.: I think maybe the most interesting question that came before the General Board during the period that I was a member, and I don't recall absolutely whether it was formally before the board as a matter for report - I can't be sure whether it was or not, but the big question did not pertain to the Navy as such. It was a question as to whether there should be established in the national defense a separate department for air. That was the principal national defense question, I think, that was in the wind during the time I was on the General Board.

Q: How did the members of your board react to that?

Adm. H.: I think that the general standpoint and opinion was that the proposition, of course, is of importance to the Navy, but as long as the Navy keeps control of its own air arm the matter is not vital to the Navy as such. It is an important national defense question, but it is not an important naval question as such. I think that was about the size of it.

Q: Was there any fear at that time among the membership of the board that if such an arm of national defense was set up it might perchance rob the Navy of its air arm?

Adm. H.: I think there was a theory that that was a possibility. I would say so, yes. I don't mean to imply that the Navy was indifferent to the matter. I think the Navy was far from being indifferent, but the Navy didn't see an immediate threat to naval air strength.

Q: Who were some of the members of the General Board when you served?

Adm. H.: It's my recollection that Admiral Hart was the senior member. If not, Admiral Hepburn was the senior member. When Admiral Hart left the board on account of having been appointed a senator from Connecticut, Admiral Hepburn was the senior member from that time on. I think there's a possibility Admiral Hepburn was the senior member before Admiral Hart departed. I can't be sure without checking the book. Because Admiral Hart left the board not very long after I joined. Admiral Hepburn was the senior member during most of the term of my membership.

Q: In your estimation, how useful was the General Board?

Adm. H.: That is a broad question, of course. I think that the General Board can be very useful to an administration that chooses to rely greatly upon its advice, and naturally of less use to an administration that's less inclined to refer to the General Board. I don't feel that my short period on the General Board was sufficient for me to form a properly considered viewpoint on that topic, for the reason that my period there was relatively short.

Q: It was eighteen months, wasn't it?

Adm. H.: It was about eighteen months, yes. It was relatively short and was during a time when the topics connected with the ongoing war were perhaps of more pressing importance than matters of long-range policy, which naturally would mean post-war policy. I think there was a feeling that change in policy during the waging of the current war was to be approached with extreme caution. I think that was the general attitude.

The General Board, of course, did not have to do with war strategy. That was well understood by all hands, I think.

Q: Did you get into the subject of demobilization, which was inevitable?

Adm. H.: No. I don't recall that we were brought to a consideration of demobilization. As a matter of fact, demobilization didn't even seem imminent until a year or more after I'd left the board.

Q: It began to be a matter of real concern in the Navy Department before the war was ended and there were many plans for what would happen once the war did end. This was in 1945 when you were on the board. That's why I asked you.

Adm. H.: I was on the board until approximately the middle of 1945. No, I don't remember that any demobilization topic was placed before the board.

Q: Did Secretary Forrestal use the board extensively?

Adm. H.: It was my impression that Secretary Forrestal did not use the board very actively. He came to the board one day for an informal sort of discussion which didn't last very long, according to my recollection, and I certainly do not recall that the Secretary ever required the board to consider and report upon demobilization, not to my recollection.

Q: I would think that a matter of new ship design and that sort of thing would be of interest to the board. Was it?

Adm. H.: Yes, that has traditionally been one of the functions of the General Board, to consider and recommend on matters pertaining to ship characteristics, numbers and types. Ships characteristics have traditionally been among the important topics considered by the General Board.

Q: It would seem that there is a place in the Navy set-up for such a board. It's been discontinued, but it would seem to me that there should be a place where the knowledge and experience and skill of outstanding naval officers who have retired could be utilized. Otherwise, it's something of a waste, is it not?

Adm. H.: Yes, unless they choose to become exponents in the press or on the lecture platform, or through some medium. I think that by and large officers who retire from the Navy have been not only reluctant but maybe even resolved not to attempt to be guiding influences after they have retired.

Q: That's understandable, but at the same time it seems to me that there's an awful lot of knowledge and experience, collectively speaking, represented in a group of retired senior officers, and it should be utilized in an official way, as the General Board was an official board.

Adm. H.: Yes. Of course, the General Board, by and large, was made up of retired officers, so those members do have a voice to that extent after they're on the retired list.

Q: But it has been discontinued, so they're no longer there.

Adm. H.: Well, that's a matter of administration policy. I don't know myself what led to the discontinuance of the Board, nor do I remember exactly when it occurred. But it had the wisdom to recommend just what changes should be made. Things were happening so fast. I don't think our board felt that we were in a position to be pundits at that time. That's my general recollection.

Q: Yes. Well, you stayed on the board actually until the war was over, did you not?

Adm. H.: No, the war was still on. My membership of the board ended on the 30th of June 1945.

In 1909 when I was a passed midshipman and serving on the USS West Virginia, the armored cruiser, one of the units of the armored cruiser squadron - in the fall of 1909 the armored cruiser squadron cruised to the Orient and back. After we left Hawaii, having been there for several weeks, our next stop was in the Admiralty Islands. Admiralty Islands, of course, are just north of New Guinea and they are inhabited by a race of people who are commonly called Papuans, I believe —

Q: Or fuzzy-wuzzies!

Adm. H.: Yes, they were the fuzzy-wuzzies of their time, I guess.

Anyhow, we stopped at Naries Harbor in the Admiralties and we stopped there long enough to make a boat survey of Naries Harbor. I was the assistant navigator on the <u>West Virginia</u> at that time so I was detailed as a member of the survey, running a sextant and giving our navigator data for his plot. On the first morning of this boat survey we approached the shore of one of the western islands of Naries Harbor and, as we approached the shore, there was a congregation of natives right down on the beach. They were not only natives, but they were native savages because they had no clothing whatever. They were all men, they all carried spears, they wore no clothing except a g-string, and an armlet on either arm, and — we found this out later — the armlets were used as pockets because through the armlets they stuck the stems of their pipes and they stuck the blades of their knives. As we cruised along the shore of this little islet with this mob, numbering, I suppose, about two dozen or so, all of a sudden they let loose with a volley of spears, which didn't do us any harm because we were probably 200 yards off and their spears maybe went 150 or something like that. It was a gesture but it was by no means a welcoming ceremony. It quite took us aback. We didn't know what to make of that.

But anyhow we went about our business and we ran our line of soundings. Our navigator, who was down in the little cabin of the steamer with his drawing board and charts set up, recording his plots, and we were back and forth taking our lines and soundings and establishing the position with landmarks which we designated more or less arbitrarily. Lunch time came along and we decided that we would take a chance and run up into a little cove which we saw looked inviting, overhung with palm trees and so on. So we ran into the little cove, dropped anchor, and went about our luncheon. Presently, natives appeared through the palm trees down on the beach. Sure enough, they were carrying spears but they didn't bother us. They just came down with their spears and looked on. So we went ahead with our lunch, of which the main element was cans of corned beef that opened with a key. I suppose there was about a pound of corned beef there in the boat as part of the lunch for half a dozen people, the boat's crew, the navigator party, and a couple of midshipmen taking sextant angles. There were perhaps seven of us, all told, so a couple of pounds of corned beef more than went around and we had something left over, so we passed that out to the

Natives who were gathered around and still scanning us. That can of corned beef still had the key that opened it.

The next day we continued with our boat survey and we anchored again in that cove for lunch and we were again surrounded by a good part of the local population, male. One of these bucks had a new departure that made him very, very stylish. Instead of sort of a skewer through the septum of his nose, he had the key that had opened the can of corned beef the day before. He was hot stuff! He had a new ornament for his nose.

That was at Naries Harbor, in the Admiralties, in the fall of 1909. In the fall of 1944, I was relieved by Oscar Badger on board the *Iowa* at Ulithi. Of course, I was bound then to report in to CinCus here in Washington, so from way out there passage was catch as catch can. But it so happened that Admiral Halsey's flag plane was due for an overhaul, and that seemed like a very good opportunity to overhaul his flag plane. So I had passage from Ulithi up to Hawaii on Halsey's flag plane, and our first stop from Ulithi was down at Manus, in the Admiralties. By that time there was an impromptu and temporary U.S. naval base at Manus, and when we got in there at Manus it developed that the flag plane would need so many hours of overhaul before she could be trusted to fly on from there. So I had an over-Sunday stop facing me at Manus and I learned at the naval Headquarters in Manus, where I was going to put up overnight that they were sending a plane - no, not a plane, a boat - the next morning to the little air station that had been set up at Naries Harbor. Gosh, that was right at home for me because I'd been at Naries Harbor 35 years previously and I thought I'd like to see what it looked like. So I got permission to go with the boat to the radio station at Naries Harbor.

Well, to make a long story short, that was an all-day expedition, but I found when we got up there at Naries Harbor that the boat on which I went up actually poked into the same little cove that we had used for our luncheon stops in 1909. I went ashore there on a little temporary wooden pier just big enough to walk on, probably twenty or twenty-five feet long. But here I was in the identical little cove where our survey boat had stopped for luncheon on two successive days in 1909 and been inspected by these savages who picked up the key of the tin can and used it for his nose and that sort of thing.

Q: I bet you halfway looked for a man with a key in his nose!

Adm. H.: I did, I looked for that man. I thought I might have identified him, but I couldn't be sure.

Q: Were they still wearing things in their noses?

Adm. H.: No, I don't think they were at that time. In the interim I think they had gone to shorts of some kind. I don't think shirts. I think they still were bare from the waist up. I saw to my surprise that a young woman came along this path and went about her business. We didn't see a woman during the two days that we stopped there for lunch.

Q: Liberation must have come down there sooner than it did up here?

Adm. H.: Yes, I'm sure.

Index to

a Series of Interviews with

Vice Admiral Olaf M. Hustvedt,

U. S. Navy (Retired)

Hustvedt

ADMIRALTY ISLANDS: visit of the WEST VIRGINIA (1909), p 27-8; visit in 1944, p 28-29; Naries Harbor in 1909, p 292 ff; Naries Harbor again in 1944, p 295.

ALEUTIANS: Fleet Exercise, p 143; p 164-5; protests entered by citizens against holding a fleet problem in the Aleutians, p 148-151.

ATLANTIC FLEET: Hustvedt serves as Chief of Staff to Commander in Chief, p 199 ff; Ingersoll takes over from Adm. King (Jan. 1942), p 221; the role of guiding and protecting shipping follows immediately upon the attack on Pearl Harbor, p 222.

USS AUGUSTA: flagship of Admiral King in 1941, p 216; Ingersol gives her up as flagship because of need for base with modern communications equipment, p 224.

BANTRY BAY: base for Division 7 of U. S. Battleships in 1918, p 57-8.

BASTEDO, Rear Admiral Paul H.: p 249-50.

BB DIVISIONS - Commander of: duties of an Aide to Commander, p 113; Hustvedt serves as gunnery officer, p 114.

BB DIVISION 7: under RADM Thos. Rodgers in 1918 based at Bantry Bay, p 57-8; in 1944 BB Div. 7 consisted of BBs IOWA and NEW JERSEY ordered to Pacific, Jan. 1944 - destination Funafuti, p 257; p 275-6; see also entries under: MILI; FAST CARRIER ATTACK FORCES; MARSHALL ISLANDS CAMPAIGN.

BERNHARD, VADM Alva D.: in command of a Task Force operating with the British Home Fleet - relieved by Hustvedt (1942), p 244; p 247-8.

BLOCH, ADM C. C.: CinC, Pacific - Hustvedt joins his staff as fleet operations officer, p 170 ff; p 179.

BONUS ARMY: p 131.

BRITISH GRAND FLEET: based at Scapa Flow in the Orkneys, p 56-7; Adm. Rodgers sends a deputation (including Hustvedt) to visit the American command with the Grand Fleet to learn about operating techniques, p 58-9.

BUREAU OF ORDNANCE: Hustvedt ordered to the Bureau after World War I (1919) as Chief of the experimental section, p 64; interest in smoke producing projectiles, p 65-7; an Experimental Ammunition Unit within the Naval Gun Factory established, p 67; Dr. Robert Goddard and his work with rockets, p 68 ff; Bureau interested in Goddard's work mainly to extend range for attack on submerged submarines, p 71, p 74; limited appropriations, p 73-4; Hustvedt alternates with Theodore Wilkinson on the experimental desk, p 75; Hustvedt returns to BuOrd (1924) after tour in Hawaiian waters, p 90 ff; the rapid change noticed in Naval Ordnance, p 91; the aircraft armament section, p 93-4; the Norden bombsight, p 94-5; other interests of the Bureau in 1924-5, p 99; interest in armament for lighter-than-aircraft, p 101-4.

USS BURNS: a unit of the mine squadron at Pearl Harbor - Hustvedt in Command, p 78, p 81, p 83-4.

Hustvedt

GREEN, CMDR Fitzhugh USNR: Attends George Washington University with Hustvedt to study organic chemistry, p 46.

HALSEY, Fleet Admiral Wm.: - 263-4.

HART, ADM Thomas C.: Flag officer in command of cruisers - LOUISVILLE serves as flagship, p 142; p 147, member of the General Board, (1944), p 287.

HAUGEN, The Hon. Gilbert: names young Hustvedt to the Naval Academy, p 10.

HAWAIIAN ISLANDS - 1909; p 35-6.

HUSTVEDT, VADM Olaf M.: Personal data, p 1-6; the Admiral's father as a clergyman, p 6-7; his uncle intercedes for him with Cong. Haugen - appointment to the Naval Academy, p 9-10; examinations for ensign, p 39, p 42; exams for promotion to Lieutenant j.g., p 49; family arrangements in Hawaii (1923), p 82; school provisions for the children, p 88-9; use of the Calvert Method for teaching in the home, p 89; family living at Long Beach (1927-30) p 140-1; the family purchases a house on Ordway Street in Washington, D. C., p 145-6; Hustvedt talks of his considerable staff officer experience, p 169 ff; recollections on his tour of duty with Cinc Block, p 179-80; the family status in 1940, p 181; selected for flag rank (Aug. 1941), p 199; detached from the NORTH CAROLINA for duty as Chief of Staff to Admiral King (Cinc, Atlantic Fleet), p 199; his son Stephen a guest on the NORTH CAROLINA for her gun trails (1941), p 205; some aspects of New York social life while the NORTH CAROLINA was berthed there, p 210; flies his flag as RADM for first time on the USS CONSTELLATION (1942), p 235; living quarters in Newport, p 236; injury to his eye (summer of 1944), p 283-5; the medical examination at Bethesda, p 286; retired by the Board, April 1, 1945, p 287; becomes a member of the General Board, p 287.

INDIAN HEAD, Maryland: Navy proving ground, p 68.

INGERSOLL, ADM Royal E.: succeeds Admiral King (Jan. 1942) as CinC, Atlantic, p 220; p 233-4.

USS IOWA - BB: Hustvedt flies his flag (BB Div. 7) in her, p 242-3; p 254; Japanese a/c scores a near hit, p 261-2; an attempted air attack on her and the NEW JERSEY off PONAPE, p 265-6; p 269-71; probably first attempt at a kamikaze attack, p 275-6; special mission off Garapan, Saipan, p 277-8.

JOHNSTON ISLAND: Hustvedt in the USS BURNS (1923) makes exploratory visit to gather hydrographic information, p 83-4.

KING, Fleet Admiral Ernest: CinC, Atlantic Fleet (1941) - Hustvedt named as his Chief of Staff, p 199; first months on job on board the CONSTELLATION at Newport, p 200; his routine at Newport, p 219; his receipt of the news of Pearl Harbor attack, p 220-1.

KNOX, The Hon. Frank - SecNav: offers Hustvedt a ride to United Kingdom from Gander, Nfld., p 245; p 248.

LANSDOWNE, Lt.CMDR Zachary: skipper of the ill-fated SHENANDOAH (1925), p 102.

LEE, VADM Willis A.: p 270, p 275.

USS LOUISVILLE: Hustvedt becomes Executive Officer (1933-35), p 140 ff; participation in fleet exercise in the Aleutians, p 143, p 164-5; the Caribbean, p 144-5; citizen protests against holding a fleet problem in the Aleutians, p 148-151.

MAJURO: occupied by allies Jan. 31, 1944, p 260-1; becomes a fleet anchorage, p 270-3.

MANUS, Admiralty Islands: U. S. Naval Base in WW II, p 295.

MARSHALL ISLANDS campaign: BB Division 7 joins carrier operation under ADM F. C. Sherman in the USS BUNKER HILL, p 259.

MILI, Marshall Islands: BB Division 7 carries out an attack, Feb. 17, 1944 - Admiral Willis Lee rides as an observer, p 270; IOWA hit by shore batteries, p 271; p 272-4.

MINE SQUADRON 2: Hustvedt has duty for 2½ years in Hawaiian waters, p 77 ff; the base at Pearl Harbor, p 79-80.

MOFFETT, ADM Wm. A.: p 93.

MORGAN, Junius: p 207.

NARIES HARBOR, Admiralty Islands: p 293; U. S. radio station there in 1944, Hustvedt visits, p 296-7.

U. S. NAVAL ACADEMY: Hustvedt appointed in 1905, p 11, p 26; first cruise in the brig, BOXER, p 14-15; the youngster cruise, p 16-17; the typhoid epidemic, p 21-22; the class of 1909 was the last to serve two years as past midshipman, p 25-6.

NAVAL AVIATION: Admiral Hustvedt's experience at the control of a plane enroute from Anacostia to Dahlgren, p 38-9.

Hustvedt

NAVAL GUN FACTORY: Experimental Ammunition Unit, p 67-8; p 107; Hustvedt assigned to the Gun Factory as Production Chief (1930-33), p 126 ff; p 132-3; cooperation with private enterprise, p 137-8; the manufacture of optical instruments, p 138-9.

NAVAL WAR COLLEGE: Hustvedt sent there in 1940, p 180 ff; his year cut short by assignment to fit out and commission the new BB NORTH CAROLINA, p 182.

NC-4: The experimental section of BuOrd develops a "float light" for use on the transatlantic flight, p 105.

NORDEN, Carl: inventor of the bombsight...Hustvedt was present for many of the early tests, p 94-5; Nordon also worked on a type of flying bomb, p 95-6.

USS NORTH CAROLINA - BB: Hustvedt called from Naval War College to commission the NORTH CAROLINA, p 182; p 187 ff; the task of commissioning, p 189-93; Hustvedt's version of the second name for the NORTH CAROLINA - the "showboat", p 194-7; Hustvedt takes the ship on shakedown to Guantanamo but is detached in August because he has been elevated to flag rank, p 198-200; de-gaussing in the Chesapeake, p 200; gun firing trails off the Newfoundland Banks, p 201-3; p 213-15.

SS NOURMAHAL: yacht of Vincent Astor, p 210-11.

NULTON, ADM Louis M.: In 1927 was Commander of Battleship Division of the Battle Fleet, p 109-110; p 113; p 119.

USS OKLAHOMA - BB: unit of Division 7 in British waters, (1918) - Hustvedt sent as gunnery officer to fill vacancy left by CMDR Caskey's death, p 61; acts as escort to the GEORGE WASHINGTON bringing President Wilson to Brest, p 62.

OLDENDORF, ADM Jesse: classmate of Hustvedt - in command of shore base at Argentia (1942), p 243-4.

USS OLYMPIA: provided the first class cruise for Hustvedt, p 20.

USS PARCHE: Submarine skippered by VADM (Red) Ramage, p 279-81.

PASSED MIDSHIPMAN: comments on status, p 42-3.

PG SCHOOL (Post Graduate): Hustvedt takes a course at George Washington University in organic chemistry, p 45; PG school at Annapolis just formed - Hustvedt and one other were only students at GWU, p 46; Hustvedt goes for practical experience to the powder factory at Indian Head, Md., p 48-9; Carnegie Steel in Pittsburg and the Experimental Station of the Bureau of Mines, p 49; Midvale Steel Company and the Army's Frankfort Arsenal (Philadelphia), p 49-50.

PHILIPPINE ISLANDS - visit in 1909: p 30.

PHILIPPINE SEA - battle of: p 275-6.

PONAPE, Caroline Islands: - 265-6.

USS RALEIGH: Hustvedt ordered to her in 1921, p 43; p 44.

USS RANGER: flagship for Task Force operating with the British Home Fleet, p 247-9; p 250-2; replenishment of the garrison on Spitzbergen, p 253.

RODGERS, RADM Thos. S.: relieves Fechtler as Division Commander of Battleships, p 56; takes his division to Europe in 1918 to operate in conjunction with the British Grand Fleet, p 56-7.

ROSYTH: The Ranger there for repairs (1942), p 249-52.

USS SHENANDOAH: The final cruise in 1925 - Hustvedt just missed that flight, p 101-4.

USS SOUTH DAKOTA - BB: hit by kamikaze in Battle of the Philippine Sea, p 276.

SPRUANCE, ADM Raymond: p 263-4.

STARK, ADM Harold: in London, p 246; p 248-50.

STUMP, ADM Felix B.: p 269; in command of the CV LEXINGTON, p 269-70; p 274.

THIRD FLEET: p 263-4.

TIJUANA, Mexico: p 39-40.

TINIAN: bombardment by BB Division 7 - part of a planned effort, p 267-8.

TORCH Operation: planning for, p 226-7; p 237-8.

TRUK: Japanese naval base in Caroline Islands - air bombardment by U. S. in early, 1944, p 260-1.

USS UTAH - BB: Hustvedt assigned to the Utah (1914), p 51 ff; becomes a turret officer, p 51; assistant fire control officer, p 53-4; detached in 1961, p 54.

VETLESON, Mrs. Unger: Supplies organ for chapel services in the BB NORTH CAROLINA, p 208, p 212.

USS VIXON: a converted yacht serves as command ship for Cinc, Atlantic, p 225; her sojourn in Hampton Roads during the planning for Operation TORCH, p 226.

USS WASHINGTON - BB: sister ship to the NORTH CAROLINA, p 195.

USS WEST VIRGINIA - armored cruiser: first duty assignment of Hustvedt (1909), p 26 ff; cruise to the orient with a stop in the Admiralty Islands, p 26-8; the Philippines, p 30; Hong Kong, p 31-2; Japan, p 34-5; p 39; Hustvedt represents the WEST VIRGINIA on an inspection trip of prisoners in Tijuana, p 40-41; p 113; p 292.

www.ingramcontent.com/pod-product-compliance
Lightning Source LLC
Chambersburg PA
CBHW082150070526
44585CB00020B/2162